# Rick Steves®
## SNAPSHOT

# Loire
# Valley

T0018802

# CONTENTS

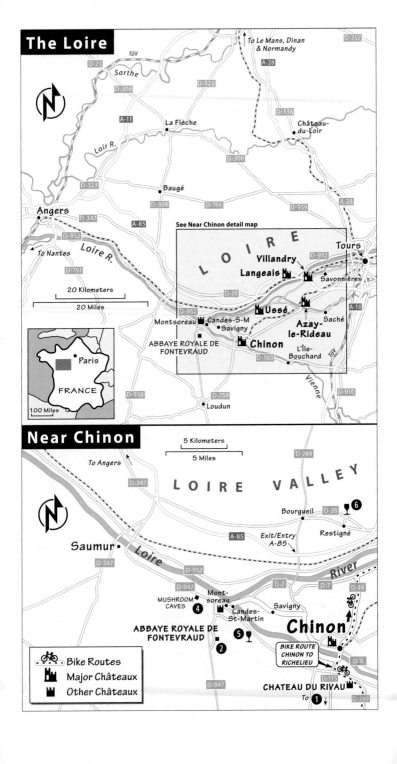

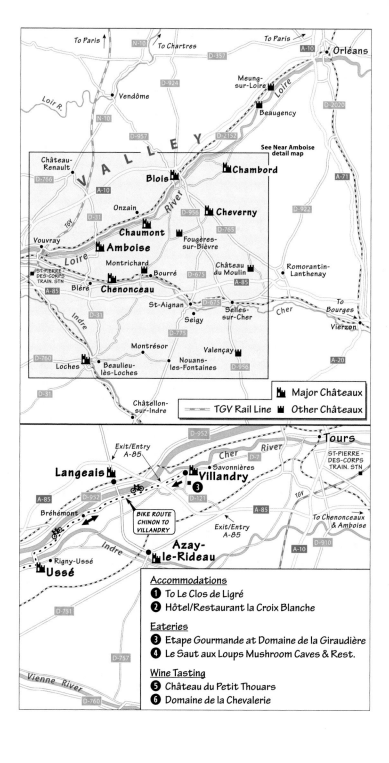

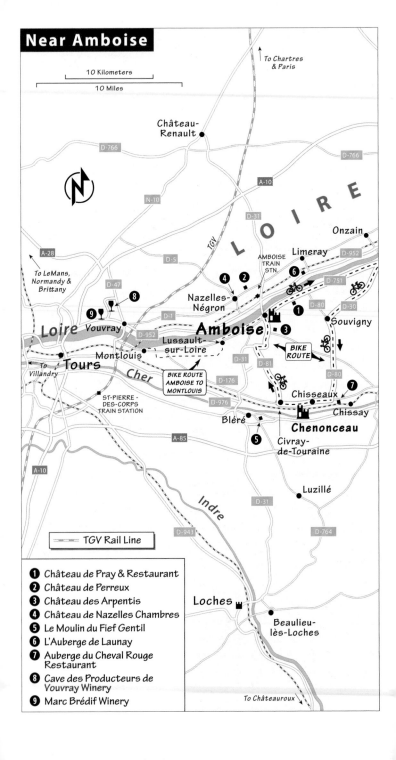

# Near Amboise

10 Kilometers

10 Miles

To Chartres & Paris

Château-Renault

D-766

A-10

N-10

D-31

TGV

D-5

L O I R E

Onzain

Limeray

D-952

AMBOISE TRAIN STN.

D-751

A-28

To LeMans, Normandy & Brittany

D-47

❹ ❷

Nazelles-Négron

❻ 🚲

D-80

Souvigny

🚲

❽

D-1

❾

Vouvray

Loire

D-952

Amboise ■ ❸

❶

D-30

🚲

Lussault-sur-Loire

BIKE ROUTE

Montlouis

To Villandry

Tours

Cher

BIKE ROUTE AMBOISE TO MONTLOUIS

D-31

D-81

D-80

🚲

Chisseaux ❼

ST-PIERRE-DES-CORPS TRAIN STATION

D-176

D-976

Chissay

Bléré

❺

Chenonceau

Civray-de-Touraine

A-85

Luzillé

A-10

Indre

D-31

D-764

D-943

TGV Rail Line

Loches

Beaulieu-lès-Loches

To Châteauroux

❶ Château de Pray & Restaurant
❷ Château de Perreux
❸ Château des Arpentis
❹ Château de Nazelles Chambres
❺ Le Moulin du Fief Gentil
❻ L'Auberge de Launay
❼ Auberge du Cheval Rouge Restaurant
❽ Cave des Producteurs de Vouvray Winery
❾ Marc Brédif Winery

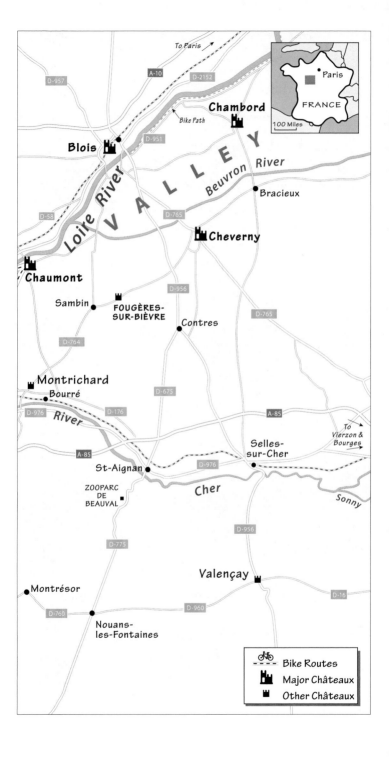

# INTRODUCTION

This Snapshot guide, excerpted from my guidebook *Rick Steves France,* is all about the Loire Valley. What was once the preserve of French aristocracy is now a playground for commoners like us. Exquisite châteaux dot the lush landscape of the Loire Valley like jewels in a crown—I cover more than a dozen of my favorites. Chenonceau delights with its dramatic setting atop a river, while the king's "hunting lodge" at Chambord astonishes with 440 rooms—and almost as many chimneys. The best gardens are at Villandry, while the immaculately preserved Cheverny has the most impressive furnishings. When you need a break, rise above it all in a hot-air balloon or get a feel for the countryside by renting a bike. A visit to "the garden of France" confirms why the Loire Valley was royalty's number-one getaway.

To help you have the best trip possible, I've included the following topics in this book:

• **Planning Your Time,** with advice on how to make the most of your limited time

• **Orientation,** including tourist information (abbreviated as TI), tips on public transportation, local tour options, and helpful hints

• **Sights,** with ratings and strategies for meaningful and efficient visits

• **Sleeping** and **Eating,** with good-value recommendations in every price range

• **Connections,** with tips on trains, buses, and driving

**Practicalities,** near the end of this book, has information on money, staying connected, hotel reservations, transportation, and other helpful hints, plus French survival phrases.

To travel smartly, read this little book in its entirety before you go. It's my hope that this guide will make your trip more meaningful and rewarding. Traveling like a temporary local, you'll get the absolute most out of every mile, minute, and dollar.

*Bon voyage!* Happy travels!

Rick Steves

# THE LOIRE

*Amboise • Chinon • Beaucoup de Châteaux*

As it glides gently east to west, officially separating northern from southern France, the Loire River has come to define this popular tourist region. The importance of this river and the valley's prime location, in the center of the country just south of Paris, have made the Loire a strategic hot potato for more than a thousand years. The Loire was the high-water mark for the Moors as they pushed into Europe from Morocco. Today, this region is still the dividing line for the country—for example, weather forecasters say, "north of the Loire...and south of the Loire..."

Because of its history, the Loire Valley is home to more than a thousand castles and palaces of all shapes and sizes. When a "valley address" became a must-have among 16th-century hunting-crazy royalty, rich Renaissance palaces replaced outdated medieval castles. Hundreds of these castles and palaces are open to visitors, and it's castles that you're here to see. Old-time aristocratic château-owners, struggling with the cost of upkeep, enjoy financial assistance from the government if they open their mansions to the public.

Today's Loire Valley is carpeted with fertile fields, crisscrossed by rivers, and laced with rolling hills. It's one of France's most important agricultural regions. The region is also under some development pressure, thanks to TGV bullet trains (also called "InOui" trains) that link it to Paris in well under two hours, and cheap flights to England that have made it a prime second-home spot for many Brits, including Sir Mick Jagger.

LOIRE

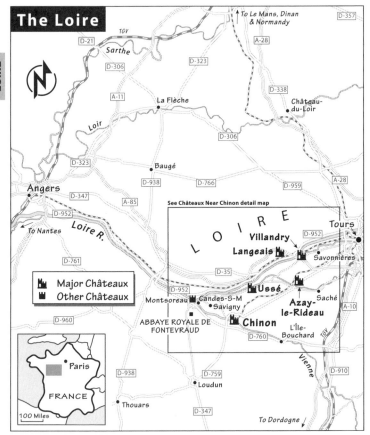

The Loire

To Le Mans, Dinan & Normandy

TGV
Sarthe
D-21
D-306
A-11
La Flèche
A-28
D-323
D-338
Château-du-Loir
D-306
Loir
D-323
Baugé
D-938    D-766    D-959    A-28
Angers
D-347
D-952
A-85
To Nantes
Loire R.
See Châteaux Near Chinon detail map
L O I R E
Tours
Villandry
D-952
Langeais
Savonnières
D-761
D-35
Major Châteaux
Other Châteaux
D-952    Ussé    Saché
Montsoreau    Candes-S-M    Azay-le-Rideau    A-10
Savigny
D-960
ABBAYE ROYALE DE FONTEVRAUD    Chinon    L'Île-Bouchard
D-760
Vienne
Paris
D-938    D-759    D-910
FRANCE    Loudun
100 Miles    Thouars    D-347
To Dordogne

## CHOOSING A HOME BASE

This is a big, unwieldy region with sights scattered far and wide, so I've divided it into two halves: east and west of the sprawling city of Tours. Each area is centered on a good, manageable town—**Amboise** (east) or **Chinon** (west)—to use as a home base for exploring nearby châteaux. Which home base should you choose? That depends on which châteaux you plan to visit; for ideas, scan the "Loire Valley Châteaux at a Glance" sidebar, later. For first-time visitors, Amboise is, hands-down, the better choice.

Châteaux-holics and gardeners can stay longer and sleep in both towns. Avoid driving across traffic-laden Tours; the A-85 autoroute (toll) is the quickest way to link Amboise with châteaux near Chinon (about an hour). Thanks to this uncrowded freeway, sleepy Azay-le-Rideau is another good base for destinations west of Tours; it also works as a base for sights on both sides.

**East of Tours: Amboise** and, to a lesser extent, **Blois** or

LOIRE

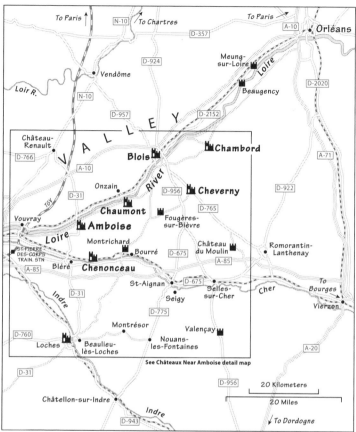

Chenonceaux, make the best home bases for this area. Amboise and Blois have handy car or bus/minivan access to these important châteaux: elegant Chenonceau, urban Blois, epic Chambord, canine-crazy Cheverny, royal Amboise, and garden-showy Chaumont-sur-Loire. Amboise has minivan service to area sights, and drivers appreciate its small scale and easy parking; Blois has better train connections from Paris and better low-cost transportation to nearby sights in high season but lacks the small-town warmth of Amboise. The peaceful village of Chenonceaux works for drivers and hardy bicyclists. Most visitors choose Amboise for its just-right size and more varied tourist appeal.

West of Tours: Chinon, Azay-le-Rideau, and their nearby châteaux don't feel as touristy; these towns appeal to gardeners and road-less-traveled types. The key châteaux in this area are historic Chinon, fairy-tale Azay-le-Rideau, fortress-like Langeais, and garden-lush Villandry. Lesser sights include the châteaux at Rivau and Ussé, plus the historic Abbaye Royale de Fontevraud. Azay-le-Rideau is best for cyclists, with convenient rental shops, good access to bike paths, and interesting destinations within pedaling distance for experienced riders.

**Château Hotels:** If ever you wanted to sleep in a castle surrounded by a forest, the Loire Valley has choices in all price ranges. Most of my "castle hotel" recommendations are best with a car and within 15 minutes of Amboise (see the "Near Amboise" section on page 29).

## PLANNING YOUR TIME

With frequent, convenient trains to Paris and a few direct runs right to Charles de Gaulle Airport, the Loire can be a good first or last stop on your French odyssey. Avoid a château blitz strategy; this region—"the garden of France"—is a pleasant place to linger.

Two full days are sufficient to sample the best châteaux. Don't go overboard. Three châteaux, possibly four, are the recommended dose. Famous châteaux are least crowded early, during lunch, and late in the day. Most open at about 9:00 and close between 18:00 and 19:00.

A day trip from Paris to the Loire is doable. Bus and minivan tours make getting to the main châteaux a breeze (see "Getting Around the Loire Valley," later).

### With a Car

For the single best day in the Loire, consider this plan: Visit Amboise's sights the afternoon of arrival, then sleep in or near Amboise. The next morning, visit my favorite château—graceful Chenonceau—arriving before 9:00 to be one of the first in. Next, drive to Cheverny (40 minutes). End your day at monumental Chambord, a 15-minute drive from Cheverny. Energetic travelers could visit Chaumont on their way back to Amboise.

With a second full day, you could move to Chinon or Azay-le-Rideau, and from there visit Villandry and its gardens, Azay-le-Rideau, and the château and old town in Chinon. These visits are also workable as a long day trip from Amboise.

Try to see one château on your drive in (for example, if arriving from the north, visit Chambord, Chaumont, or Blois; if coming from the west or the south, see Azay-le-Rideau or Villandry). If you're coming from Burgundy, don't miss the one-of-a-kind Château de Guédelon. If you're driving to the Dordogne from the Loire, the A-20 autoroute via Limoges (near Oradour-sur-Glane) is fastest and toll-free until Brive-la-Gaillarde.

The best map of the area is Michelin #518, covering all the sights in this chapter. The Tours TI's free map of Touraine—the area surrounding Tours—is also good.

## Without a Car

Sleep in Amboise and take a minivan excursion (see the next section). This is easily the best plan for most visitors and allows easy access to all châteaux described in this chapter.

Budget travelers with one day can catch the public bus or train from Amboise to the village of Chenonceaux, tour its château, then return to Amboise in the afternoon to enjoy its château and Leonardo's last stand at Clos-Lucé. With a second day, take the short (and cheap) train ride to Blois; from here, visit massive Chambord and classy Cheverny (using the château bus or renting a bike to see Chambord). Try to budget time to also visit Blois itself before returning to Amboise. With more time, those connecting Paris with Amboise or Chinon can stop in Blois en route (lockers available near the station and at Blois château).

Minivan excursions from Tours are the best option for most nondrivers staying in Chinon. Budget travelers based in Chinon or Azay-le-Rideau might consider taking an e-bike to Langeais, Ussé, and Villandry (better from Azay), as train connections are challenging.

## GETTING AROUND THE LOIRE VALLEY

Traveling by car is most efficient, and day rentals are reasonable. Trains, a few buses, minivan tours, taxis, and bikes allow those without a car to reach the well-known châteaux. Even the less famous châteaux are accessible by taxi, custom minivan excursion (affordable for small groups), or bike.

## By Car

You can rent a car most easily at the St-Pierre-des-Corps TGV station just outside Tours; rentals are also available in Amboise (see page 17) and Blois (see page 45). Parking is free at all châteaux except Chambord and Clos-Lucé.

## By Train

With easy access from Amboise and Chinon, the big city of Tours is the transport hub for travelers bent on using trains or buses to explore the Loire (but I wouldn't sleep there). Tours has two important train stations and a major bus station (with service to several châteaux). The main train station is Tours SNCF; the smaller, suburban TGV station (located between Tours and Amboise) is St-Pierre-des-Corps. The châteaux of Amboise, Blois, Chenonceau, Chaumont, Langeais, Chinon, and Azay-le-Rideau all have decent train and/or bus service from Tours' main SNCF station. Some châteaux require hefty walks from their stations; look under each sight for specifics.

LOIRE

# Loire Valley Châteaux at a Glance

Which châteaux should you visit? Here's a quick summary. Local TIs sell bundled tickets that can save you money and time (see page 16).

## Châteaux East of Tours

▲▲▲**Chenonceau** Elegant château arching over the Cher River, with lovely gardens. **Hours:** Daily 9:00-19:00, closes earlier off-season. See page 36.

▲▲▲**Chambord** Epic grandeur (440 rooms) and fun rooftop views in an evocative setting surrounded by a forest. **Hours:** Daily 9:00-18:00, Oct-March until 17:00. See page 53.

▲▲**Blois** Urban château with a beautiful courtyard and fun sound-and-light show. **Hours:** Daily April-Oct 9:00-18:30, Nov-March until 17:00. See page 44.

▲▲**Cheverny** Intimate-feeling château with lavish furnishings. **Hours:** Daily 9:15-18:30, Nov-March 10:00-17:00. See page 58.

▲▲**Chaumont-sur-Loire** Imposing setting over the Loire River, notable for its historic connections to America and impressive Festival of Gardens. **Hours:** Daily mid-April-Sept 10:00-19:30, Oct-mid-Nov until 18:00, mid-Nov-mid-April until 17:00. See page 60.

▲**Amboise** Supposed burial place of Leonardo da Vinci, with ter-

## By Bus or Minivan Tour

Buses and minivan tours offer affordable transportation to many of the valley's châteaux. Buses connect Amboise, Tours, or Blois with a handful of châteaux in peak season, and minivan tours combine several châteaux into a painless day tour.

**By Bus:** Between April and October, a bus does a loop route connecting Blois, Chambord, Cheverny, Villesavin, and Beauregard, allowing visits to the châteaux with your pick of return times (€6, see "Blois Connections" on page 52). Buses also connect

rific views over Amboise. **Hours:** Daily 9:00-18:00, July-Aug until 20:00, shorter hours Nov-March. See page 13.

▲**Clos-Lucé** In Amboise, Leonardo da Vinci's final home and gardens, with models of his creations. **Hours:** Daily 9:00-19:00, July-Aug until 20:00; shorter hours Nov-Jan. See page 21.

## Châteaux West of Tours

▲▲**Azay-le-Rideau** Set on a romantic reflecting pond, with a fairy-tale facade and beautifully furnished rooms. **Hours:** Daily 9:30-18:00, July-Aug until 19:00, Oct-March 10:00-17:15. See page 76.

▲▲**Villandry** Average palace boasting the best gardens in the Loire—and possibly all of France. **Hours:** Mid-Feb-Oct daily 9:00-18:00, Nov-mid-Feb 10:00-17:00. See page 82.

▲**Langeais** Fortress-like setting above an appealing little village with evocative 15th- and 16th-century rooms. **Hours:** Daily July-Aug 9:00-19:00, April-June and Sept-mid-Nov 9:30-18:30, mid-Nov-March 10:00-17:00. See page 80.

▲**Abbaye Royale de Fontevraud** 12th-century abbey complex with a magnificent church and an excellent museum of modern art. **Hours**: Daily 9:30-19:00, Nov-March until 18:00, closed Jan. See page 84.

Tours, Amboise, and Chenonceaux (see "Amboise Connections" on page 33).

**By Minivan Tour:** Several tour operators offer half- and full-day itineraries from Amboise or Tours that include all the main châteaux. Most of these services depart from local TIs (who can book tours for you). You'll save time (in line) and money (on admissions) when you purchase a discounted château ticket from the driver. For specifics and pricing, see "Amboise Connections" on page 33.

**LOIRE**

## By Taxi

Taxi excursions can be affordable—particularly when split among several people and especially from the Blois train station to nearby châteaux, or from Amboise to Chenonceau. Most other châteaux are too expensive to visit by cab. For details, see "Blois Connections" on page 52, and "Amboise Connections" on page 33.

## By Bike

Cycling options are endless in the Loire, and a full range of bikes are available to rent (figure €40/day for an e-bike, and half that for a standard bike). Amboise, Chenonceaux, Blois, Azay-le-Rideau, and Chinon all make good biking bases and have rental options. A network of nearly 200 miles of bike paths and well-signed country lanes connect many châteaux near Amboise. Pick up the free bike-path map at any TI, buy the more detailed map also available at TIs, or study the route options at LoireByBike.co.uk. Your bike rental company will be able to advise you as well.

About five miles from Chinon, an extensive bike path runs along the Loire River, passing by Ussé and Langeais. It meets the Cher River at Villandry and continues along the Cher to Tours and beyond. To follow this route, get the *La Loire à Vélo* brochure at any area TI.

**Détours de Loire** can help you plan your bike route. They can also deliver rental bikes to most places in the Loire for reasonable rates. They will shuttle luggage to your next stop if you reserve ahead. They have shops in Blois and Tours, allowing one-way rentals between these and their partner shops (www.detoursdeloire.com).

## TOURS IN THE LOIRE VALLEY

**Local Guides:** An expert in all things Loire, **Fabrice Maret** lives in Blois but can meet you in Amboise to give an excellent walking tour of the city and its sights, or guide you around the area's châteaux using your rental car (€280/day plus transportation from Blois, +33 2 54 70 19 59, www.chateauxloire.com, info@chateauxloire.com).

**Aurzelle da Silva** is another good guide for this region, with similar rates (+33 6 27 29 24 52, www.loirepassionguide.fr, aurzelle.guide@gmail.com).

To experience the Loire Valley off the beaten path, consider **Loire Valley à la Carte,** where passionate and longtime resident Catherine Canteau Cohen can organize or guide your day from soup to nuts (+33 7 81 61 19 58, www.loirevalleyalacarte.com, contact@loirevalleyalacarte.com).

# Hot-Air Balloon Rides

In France's most popular regions, you'll find hot-air balloon companies eager to take you for a ride (Burgundy, the Loire,

Dordogne, and Provence are best suited for ballooning). It's not cheap, but it's unforgettable—a once-in-a-lifetime chance to sail serenely over châteaux, canals, vineyards, Romanesque churches, and villages. Balloons don't go above 3,000 feet and usually fly much lower than that, so you get a bird's-eye view of France's sublime landscapes.

Most companies offer similar deals and work this way: Trips range from 45 to 90 minutes of air time, to which you should add two hours for preparation, Champagne toast, and transport back to your starting point. Deluxe trips add a gourmet picnic, making it a four-hour event. Allow about €200 for a short tour, and about €300 for longer flights. Departures are, of course, weather-dependent, and are usually scheduled first thing in the morning or in early evening. If you've booked ahead and the weather turns bad, you can reschedule your flight, but you can't get your money back. Ask about bad-weather refund guarantees (usually around €25); unless your itinerary is very loose, it's a good idea.

Flight season is April through October. It's smart to bring a jacket for the breeze, though temperatures in the air won't differ too much from those on the ground. Heat from the propane flames that power the balloon may make your hair stand up—I wear a cap. Airsickness is usually not a problem, as the ride is typically slow and even. Baskets have no seating, so count on standing the entire trip. Group (and basket) size can vary from 4 to 16 passengers. Area TIs have brochures.

**France Montgolfières** gets good reviews and offers flights in the areas that I recommend (+33 3 80 97 38 61, US tel. 917 310 0783, www.france-balloons.com). Others are Aérocom Montgolfière (+33 2 54 33 55 00, www.aerocom.fr) and Touraine Montgolfière (+33 2 47 30 10 80, www.touraine-montgolfiere.fr).

## THE LOIRE VALLEY'S CUISINE SCENE

Here in "the garden of France," locally produced food is delicious. Look for seasonal vegetables, such as white and green asparagus, and *champignons de Paris*—mushrooms grown in local caves, not in the capital. Around Chinon, pears and apples are preserved *tapées* (dried and beaten flat for easier storage), rehydrated in alcohol, and served in tasty recipes. Loire Valley rivers yield fresh trout *(truite)*, shad *(alose)*, and smelt *(éperlan)*, which are often served fried *(friture)*. Various dishes highlight *rillons*, big chunks of cooked pork, while *rillettes*, a stringy pile of *rillons*, make for a cheap, mouthwatering sandwich spread (add a baby pickle, called a *cornichon*).

Locally raised pork is a staple, but don't be surprised to see steak, snails, *confit de canard* (a Dordogne duck specialty), and seafood on menus—the Loire borrows much from neighboring regions. The area's wonderful goat cheeses include Crottin de Chavignol (*crottin* means horse dung, which is what this cheese, when aged, resembles), Saint-Maure de Touraine (soft and creamy), and Selles-sur-Cher (mild). For dessert, try a delicious *tarte tatin* (upside-down caramel-apple tart). Regional pastries include *sablés* (shortbread cookies) from Sablé-sur-Sarthe.

## WINES OF THE LOIRE

Loire wines are overlooked, and that's a shame. The Loire is France's third-largest producer of wine and grows the greatest variety of any region. Four main grapes are grown in the Loire: two reds (gamay and cabernet franc) and two whites (sauvignon blanc and chenin blanc).

The Loire is divided into four subareas, and the name of a wine (its *appellation*) generally refers to where its grapes were grown. The Touraine subarea covers the wines of Chinon and Amboise. Using 100 percent cabernet franc grapes, growers in Chinon and Bourgeuil are the main (and best) producers of reds. Thanks to soil variation and climate differences year in and out, wines made from a single grape have an intriguing range in taste. The best white wines are the Sancerres (my opinion), made on the less-touristed eastern edge of the Loire. Less expensive, but still tasty, are Touraine Sauvignons and the sweeter Vouvray, whose *chenin blanc* grapes are grown not far from Amboise. Vouvray is also famous for its light and refreshing sparkling wines (called *vins pétillants*)—locals will tell you the only proper way to begin any meal in this region is with a glass of it, and I can't disagree (try the *rosé pétillant* for a fresh sensation). A dry rosé is popular in the Loire in the summer and can be made from a variety of grapes.

You'll pass scattered vineyards as you travel between châteaux, though there's no scenic wine road to speak of (the closest thing is around Bourgueil). It's best to call ahead before visiting a winery.

# East of Tours

The area east of Tours includes the good home-base towns of Amboise and Blois (each with their own châteaux), and several of the area's top châteaux: popular Chenonceau (in the town of Chenonceaux—another fine home base), massive Chambord, lavish Cheverny, and the strategically located up-a-cliff Chaumont.

# Amboise

Straddling the widest stretch of the Loire River, Amboise is an inviting town with a pleasing old quarter below its hilltop château. A

castle has overlooked the Loire from Amboise since Roman times. Leonardo da Vinci retired here...just one more of his many brilliant ideas.

As the royal residence of François I (r. 1515-1547), Amboise wielded far more importance than you'd imagine from a lazy walk through its center. In fact, its residents are pretty conservative, giving the town an attitude—as if no one told them they're no longer the second capital of France. Locals keep their wealth to themselves; consequently, many grand mansions hide behind nondescript facades.

With or without a car, Amboise is an ideal small-town home base for exploring the best of château country.

## Orientation to Amboise

Amboise (pop. 14,000) covers ground on both sides of the Loire, with the "Golden Island" (Ile d'Or) in the middle. The train station is north of the Loire, but nearly everything else is on the south (château) side. Pedestrian-friendly Rue Nationale parallels the river a few blocks inland and leads from the base of Château d'Amboise through the town center and past the clock tower—once part of the town wall—to the Romanesque Church of St-Denis.

### TOURIST INFORMATION

The information-packed TI is on Quai du Général de Gaulle (April-June and Sept-Oct Mon-Sat 9:30-18:00, Sun 10:00-13:00 & 14:00-17:00; July-Aug Mon-Sat 9:00-19:00, Sun 10:00-18:00; Nov-March shorter hours Mon-Sat, closed Sun; +33 2 47 57 09 28,

LOIRE

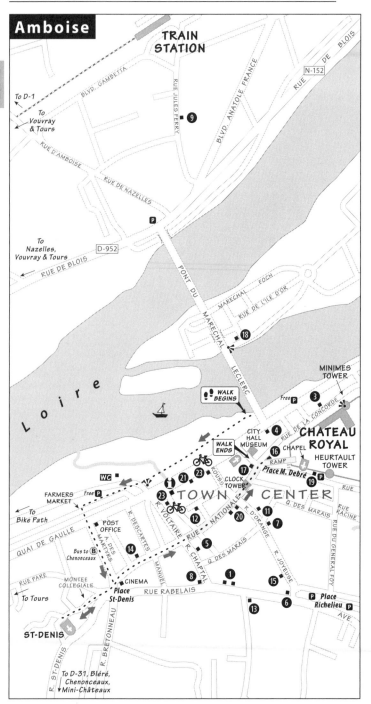

# Amboise

TRAIN STATION

To D-1

To Vouvray & Tours

BLVD. GAMBETTA

RUE D'AMBOISE

RUE DE NAZELLES

RUE JULES FERRY

BLVD. ANATOLE FRANCE

RUE DE BLOIS

N-152

**9**

To Nazelles, Vouvray & Tours

D-952

RUE DE BLOIS

PONT DU MARECHAL

MARECHAL FOCH

RUE DE L'ILE D'OR

**18**

LECLERC

MINIMES TOWER

Loire

👣 WALK BEGINS

Free P

**3**

RUE DE LA CONCORDE

CITY HALL MUSEUM

**4**

CHATEAU ROYAL

WALK ENDS

**16**

CHAPEL

HEURTAULT TOWER

**17**

CLOCK TOWER

Place M. Debré

**19**

P

RUE

WC

Free P

🚲 **23**

ℹ **21**

**23** 🚲

TOWN CENTER

R. ROUSS.

RUE NATIONALE

R. D'ORANGE

Q. DES MARAIS

RUE RACINE

FARMERS MARKET

To Bike Path

POST OFFICE

R. DESCARTES

R. VOLTAIRE

R. CHAPTAL

**12**

**20**

**11**

**7**

RUE DU GENERAL FOY

QUAI DE GAULLE

Bus to Chenonceaux

**B**

R. DES MARTYRS

R. MANUEL

**14**

**5**

Q. DES MARAIS

R. JOYEUSE

RUE PARC

MONTEE COLLEGIALE

To Tours

CINEMA

Place St-Denis

**8**

RUE RABELAIS

**1**

**15**

**13**

**6**

P Place Richelieu

P

AVE.

ST-DENIS

R. ST-DENIS

R. BRETONNEAU

To D-31, Bléré, Chenonceaux, Mini-Châteaux

LOIRE

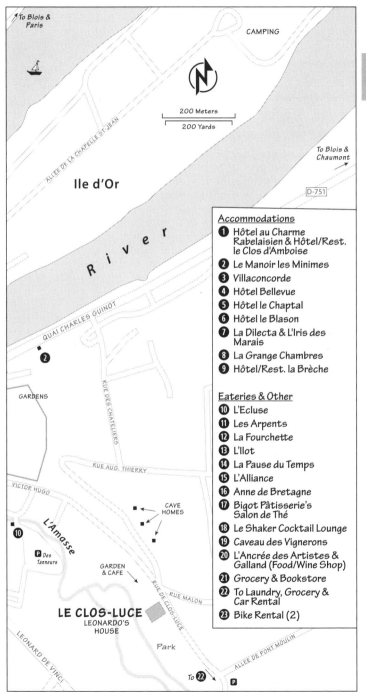

To Blois & Paris

CAMPING

200 Meters
200 Yards

To Blois & Chaumont

ALLÉE DE LA CHAPELLE ST-JEAN

Ile d'Or

D-751

River

QUAI CHARLES GUINOT

GARDENS

RUE DES CHATELIERS

RUE AUG. THIERRY

VICTOR HUGO

L'Amasse

CAVE HOMES

P Des Tanneurs

GARDEN & CAFE

RUE DE CLOS-LUCE

RUE MALON

LE CLOS-LUCE
LEONARDO'S HOUSE

Park

LEONARD DE VINCI

ALLÉE DE PONT MOULIN

To 22

P

### Accommodations
1. Hôtel au Charme Rabelaisien & Hôtel/Rest. le Clos d'Amboise
2. Le Manoir les Minimes
3. Villaconcorde
4. Hôtel Bellevue
5. Hôtel le Chaptal
6. Hôtel le Blason
7. La Dilecta & L'Iris des Marais
8. La Grange Chambres
9. Hôtel/Rest. la Brèche

### Eateries & Other
10. L'Ecluse
11. Les Arpents
12. La Fourchette
13. L'Ilot
14. La Pause du Temps
15. L'Alliance
16. Anne de Bretagne
17. Bigot Pâtisserie's Salon de Thé
18. Le Shaker Cocktail Lounge
19. Caveau des Vignerons
20. L'Ancrée des Artistes & Galland (Food/Wine Shop)
21. Grocery & Bookstore
22. To Laundry, Grocery & Car Rental
23. Bike Rental (2)

www.amboise-valdeloire.com). Pick up the city map, and consider purchasing tickets to key area châteaux (see "Helpful Hints," later). Ask about sound-and-light events at the Château Royal.

The TI can recommend local guides and help you organize tours to the châteaux with a bus or minivan service. All minivan tours from Amboise leave from the TI.

## ARRIVAL IN AMBOISE

**By Train:** Amboise's train station is birds-chirping peaceful. You can't store bags here, but you can store them at a bike shop near the TI (see "Helpful Hints," later) and at most châteaux. Allow 20 minutes to walk to the TI from the station: Turn left out of the station (you may have to cross under the tracks first), make a quick right, and walk down Rue Jules Ferry five minutes to the end, then turn right and cross the long bridge leading over the Loire River to the town center. It's a €10 taxi ride from the station to central Amboise, but taxis seldom wait at the station (see "Helpful Hints" for taxi phone numbers).

**By Car:** Drivers set their sights on the flag-festooned château that caps the hill. Parking is metered in the center of town but free in lots and along streets nearby (the big parking area downriver from the TI has lots of free parking, handy for day-trippers).

## HELPFUL HINTS

**Save Time and Money:** The TI sells tickets to sights and châteaux around Amboise and Chinon, which saves a bit on entry fees— and, more important, time spent in line. Choose the sights you want, and get tickets here. You may also get discounted tickets if you take a minivan tour (see "Getting Around the Loire Valley," earlier).

**Market Days:** Popular open-air markets are held on Friday (smaller but more local) and Sunday (the big one) in the parking lot across from the TI on the river (both 8:30-13:00). Smaller evening markets unfold near the TI or on Place St-Denis on Tuesdays in summer.

**Regional Products: Galland,** at 29 Rue Nationale, sells fine food and wine products from the Loire (daily 9:30-19:00).

**Bookstore: Lu & Approuvé** has a big selection of maps and the Michelin Green Guide *Châteaux of the Loire* in English (Mon-Sat 8:00-19:00, Sun 9:30-12:30, a block from the TI at 5 Quai du Général de Gaulle).

**Baggage Storage:** Store your bags for a small fee a few steps from the TI at **Roue Lib** bike shop (see below under "Bike Rental"). Most châteaux offer free bag storage if you've paid admission.

**Laundry:** The nearest launderette is at the **E. Leclerc supermarket,** on the outskirts of town on Avenue Léonard de Vinci.

**Supermarket:** Near the TI, **Carrefour City** is open long hours and on Sundays (at 5 Quai du Général de Gaulle), though the specialty shops on pedestrian-only Rue Nationale are infinitely more pleasing.

**Bike Rental: Roue Lib** has the best equipment for adults and kids, and is eager to help. They also have a shop in Tours, allowing for easy one-way rentals (daily 9:00-19:00, 9 Allée Sergent Turpin, +33 6 76 53 52 13, http://rouelib.eu). Another option is **Locacycle** (daily, 9:00-12:30 & 14:00-19:00, full-day rentals can be returned the next morning, 2 Rue Jean-Jacques Rousseau, +33 2 47 57 00 28, www.locacycle-amboise.fr).

**Taxi:** There's no taxi station, so you must call for one (+33 2 47 57 13 53, mobile +33 6 12 92 70 46, +33 2 47 57 30 39, or mobile +33 6 88 02 44 10).

**Car Rental:** It's easiest to rent cars at the **St-Pierre-des-Corps train station** (TGV service from Paris), a 15-minute drive from Amboise, or in Blois (see page 45).

Two other car-rental options are a €10 taxi ride away, on the outskirts of Amboise. **Europcar** is at the Total gas station at the intersection of Boulevard St-Denis Hors and Route de Chenonceaux (+33 2 47 57 07 64, www.europcar.fr). The **E. Leclerc** supermarket rents cars at reasonable rates (Avenue Léonard de Vinci, +33 2 47 30 18 57). Both are closed Sun.

**Tourist Train:** The *petit train,* with hourly departures from the TI, makes a 40-minute circuit around the city and is useful as a way to reach Clos-Lucé (€7, in peak season runs Mon-Sat 11:00-17:00, Sun from 14:00).

## Amboise Walk

This short, self-guided walk starts at the banks of the Loire River, winds past the old church of St-Denis, and meanders through the heart of town to a fine little city museum. You'll end near the entrance to Château Royal d'Amboise and Leonardo's house. Use this chapter's "Amboise" map to orient yourself.

• *Climb to the top of the embankment overlooking the river from near the bridge.*

**Amboise Riverbank:** Survey the town and its island, bridge, and castle (see "Sights in Amboise," later, to learn more about the castle). If you have a passion for anything French—philosophy, history, food, wine—you'll feel it here, along the Loire. This river, the longest in the country and the natural boundary between northern and southern France, is the last untamed river in the country (there are no dams or mechanisms to control periodic flooding, and the riverfronts are left wild). The region's châteaux line up along the Loire and its tributaries, because before trains and trucks, stones for big buildings were best shipped by boat. You may see a few of the traditional flat-bottomed Loire boats moored here. The bridge spanning the river isn't just any bridge. It marks a strategic river crossing and a longtime political border. That's why the first Amboise castle was built here. In the 15th century, this was one of the biggest forts in France.

The half-mile-long "Golden Island" (Ile d'Or) is the only island in the Loire substantial enough to withstand flooding and to have permanent buildings (including a soccer stadium, hostel, and 13th-century church). It was important historically as the place where northern and southern France came together. Truces were made here.

• *Walk downstream on the footpath above busy Quai du Général de Gaulle. After about a quarter-mile, you'll see a parking lot below and to your right, where a farmers market takes place on Friday and Sunday mornings. Drop down the steps just before the gazebo and cross the busy street. Turn left up Avenue des Martyrs de la Résistance (at the post office), then right at Place St-Denis to find the old church standing proudly on a rise to the right.*

**Church of St-Denis** (Eglise St-Denis): Ever since ancient Romans erected a Temple of Mars here, this has been a place of worship. According to legend, God sent a bolt of lightning that knocked down the statue of Mars, and Christians took over the spot. The current Romanesque church dates from the 12th century. A cute little statue of St. Denis (above the entry's arch) greets you as you step in. The delightful carvings capping the many columns inside date from Romanesque times. The lovely pastel-painted *Deposition* to the right of the choir is restored to its 16th-century brilliance. The medieval stained glass in the windows, likely destroyed in the French Revolution, was replaced with 19th-century glass. A plaque in the rear of the church lists Amboise residents who died in World War I.

From the steps of the church, look out to the hill-capping Amboise château. For a thousand years, it's been God on this hill and the king on that one. It's interesting to think how, throughout French history, the king's power generally trumped the Church's, and how the Church and the king worked to keep people down—setting the stage for the French Revolution.

• *Retrace your steps down from the church and across Place St-Denis, go past Amboise's cinema, continue walking straight, and follow Rue Nationale through the heart of town toward the castle.*

**Rue Nationale:** In France, districts around any castle or church officially classified as historic are preserved. The broad, pedestrianized Rue Nationale, with its narrow intersecting lanes, survives from the 15th century. At that time, when the town spread at the foot of the king's castle, this was the "Champs-Elysées" of Amboise. Supporting the king and his huge entourage was a serious industry. The French king spilled money wherever he stayed.

As you walk along this spine of the town, spot rare surviving bits of rustic medieval oak in the half-timbered buildings. The homes of wealthy merchants rose from the chaos of this street. Side lanes can be more candid—they often show what's hidden behind modern facades.

Stop when you reach the impressive **clock tower** (Tour de l'Horloge), built into part of the 15th-century town wall. This was once a fortified gate, opening onto the road to the city of Tours. Imagine the hefty wood-and-iron portcullis (fortified door) that dropped from above.

• *At the intersection with Rue François I (where you'll be tempted by the Bigot chocolate shop), turn left a couple of steps to the...*

**City Hall Museum:** This free museum is worth a quick peek for its romantic interior, town paintings, and historic etchings (a flier gives some English explanations, inconsistent hours, usually open July-Aug daily 10:00-12:30 & 14:00-19:00, otherwise closed). In the room dedicated to Leonardo da Vinci are his busts and photos of the gripping deathbed painting of him with caring King François I at his side (the original is on loan to the château). In the Salle des Rois (Kings' Room), find portraits of Charles VIII (who coldcocked himself at Amboise's castle; more on this later) and other nobles; I like to admire their distinct noses.

Upstairs, in the still-functioning city assembly hall (last room), notice how the photo of the current president faces the lady of the Republic. (According to locals, her features change with the taste of the generation, and the bust of France's Lady Liberty is often modeled on famous supermodels of the day.)

• *Retrace your steps along Rue François I to **Place Michel Debré**, at the base of the Château Royal d'Amboise and the end of this walk. Here, at one of the most touristy spots in the Loire, tourism's importance to the local economy is palpable. Notice the fat, round 15th-century fortified tower, whose interior ramp was built for galloping horses to spiral up to castle level (but without a horse, you'll have to walk up the long ramp). Beyond the château is Leonardo's last residence at Clos-Lucé.*

# Sights in Amboise

## CHATEAUX
### ▲Château Royal d'Amboise
This historic heap, built mostly in the late 15th century, became the favored royal residence in the Loire under Charles VIII. Charles is famous for accidentally killing himself by walking into a door lintel

on his way to a tennis match (seriously). Later, more careful occupants include Louis XII (who moved the royal court to Blois) and François I (who physically brought the Renaissance here in 1516, in the person of Leonardo da Vinci).

**Cost and Hours:** €13.50, daily 9:00-18:00, July-Aug until 20:00, shorter hours Nov-March, includes multimedia guide, Place Michel Debré, +33 2 47 57 00 98, www.chateau-amboise. com. The château offers evening events at various times during the year (see "Other Sights and Activities," later). There's a nice café with snack and lunch options on-site.

**Visiting the Château:** After climbing the long ramp to the ticket booth, your first stop is the petite **chapel** where Leonardo da Vinci is supposedly buried. This flamboyant little Gothic chapel is where the king began and ended each day in prayer. It comes with two fireplaces "to comfort the king" and two plaques "evoking the final resting place" of Leonardo (one in French, the other in Italian). Where he's actually buried, no one seems to know. Look up at the ceiling to appreciate the lacy design.

Enter the **castle rooms** across from Leonardo's chapel. The three-floor route takes you chronologically from Gothic-style rooms to those from the early Renaissance and on to the 19th century. The first room, **Salle des Gardes,** shows the château's original, much larger size; drawings in the next room give you a better feel for its original look. Some wings added in the 15th and 16th centuries have disappeared. (The little chapel you just saw was once part of the bigger complex.)

You'll pass the sumptuous **council chambers** (Salle du Conseil) where the king would meet with his key staff (find his throne). King **Henry II's bedroom** is livable. The second son of François I, Henry is remembered as the husband of the ambitious and unscrupulous Catherine de' Medici—and for his tragic death in a jousting tournament.

The rose-colored top-floor rooms are well furnished from the post-Revolutionary 1800s and demonstrate the continued interest among French nobility in this château. Find the classy portrait of King Louis-Philippe, the last Louis to rule France.

The **Minimes Tower** delivers grand views from its terrace. From here, the strategic value of this site is clear: The visibility is great, and the river below provided a natural defense.

The bulky tower climbs 130 feet in five spirals—designed for a mounted soldier in a hurry. Walk a short distance down the spiral ramp and exit into the **gardens.** Each summer, bleachers are set up for sound-and-light spectacles—a faint echo of the extravaganzas Leonardo orchestrated for the court. Modern art decorating the garden reminds visitors of the inquisitive and scientific Renaissance spirit that Leonardo brought to town. The flags are those of France and Brittany—a reminder that, in a sense, modern France was created at the nearby château of Langeais when Charles VIII (who was born here) married Anne of Brittany, adding her domain to the French kingdom.

Spiral down the **Heurtault Tower** (through the gift shop). As with the castle's other tower, this was designed to accommodate a soldier on horseback. As you gallop down to the exit, notice the cute little characters and scenes left by 15th-century stone carvers. While they needed to behave when decorating churches and palaces, here they could be a bit racier and more spirited.

**Leaving the Château:** The turnstile puts you on the road to Château du Clos-Lucé (described next; turn left and hike straight for 10 minutes). Along the way, you'll pass **troglodyte houses**—both new and old—carved into the hillside stone (a type called *tuffeau,* a sedimentary rock). Originally, poor people resided here—the dwellings didn't require expensive slate roofing, came with natural insulation, and could be dug essentially for free, as builders valued the stone quarried in the process. Today wealthy stone lovers are renovating them into stylish digs worthy of *Better Homes and Caves.* You can see chimneys high above. Unfortunately, none are open to the public.

### ▲Château du Clos-Lucé and Leonardo da Vinci Park

In 1516, Leonardo da Vinci packed his bags (and several of his favorite paintings, including the *Mona Lisa*) and left an imploding Rome for better wine and working conditions in the Loire Valley. He accepted the position of engineer, architect, and painter to France's Renaissance king, François I. This "House of Light" is the plush palace where Leonardo spent his last three years. (He died on May 2, 1519.) François,

only 22 years old, installed the 65-year-old Leonardo here just so he could enjoy his intellectual company.

The house is a kind of fort-château of its own, with a fortified rampart walk and a 16th-century chapel. Two floors of finely decorated rooms are open to the public, but most of the furnishings are neither original nor compelling (though you can stare face-to-face at a copy of Leonardo's *Mona Lisa* and see a re-creation of the artist's studio and study). Come here to learn about the genius of Leonardo and to see well-explained models of his inventions, displayed inside the house and out in the huge park.

Leonardo attracted disciples who stayed active here, using this house as a kind of workshop and laboratory. The place survived the Revolution because the quick-talking noble who owned it was sympathetic to the cause; he convinced the Revolutionaries that, philosophically, Leonardo would have been on their side.

**Cost and Hours:** The €18 admission (includes house and gardens) is worth it for Leonardo fans with two hours to fully appreciate this sight. Skip the special exhibit (*Da Vinci et la France,* in the garden) and its €5 supplement. Open daily 9:00-19:00, July-Aug until 20:00, shorter hours Nov-Jan, last entry one hour before closing, +33 2 47 57 00 73, www.vinci-closluce.com.

**Getting There:** It's a 10-minute walk uphill at a steady pace from Château Royal d'Amboise, past troglodyte homes (see end of previous listing). You can also take the *petit train* (listed under "Helpful Hints," earlier). If you park in the nearby lot, leave nothing of value visible in your car.

**Tours:** Follow the helpful free English handout. A free app in English includes background information and audio tours of the château and grounds.

**Eating:** Several garden cafés, including one just behind the house and others in the park, are reasonably priced and appropriately meditative. For a view over Amboise, choose the terrace *crêperie* just behind the château.

**Visiting the Château and Gardens:** Your visit begins with a tour of Leonardo's elegant yet livable Renaissance **home.** This little residence was built in 1450—just within the protective walls of the town—as a guesthouse for the king's château nearby. Today it re-creates (with Renaissance music) the everyday atmosphere Leonardo enjoyed while he lived here, pursuing his passions to the very end. Find the touching sketch in Leonardo's bedroom of François I comforting his genius pal on his deathbed.

The basement level is filled with **sketches** recording the storm patterns of Leonardo's brain and **models** of his remarkable inventions (inspired by nature and built according to his notes). Helpful descriptions—written and visual—reveal his vision for these way-before-their-time inventions. Leonardo was fascinated by water. All he lacked was steam power. It's hard to imagine that this Roman candle of creativity died nearly 500 years ago. Imagine Leonardo's résumé letter to kings of Europe: "I can help your armies by designing tanks, flying machines, wind-up cars, gear systems, extension ladders, and water pumps." The French considered him a futurist who never really implemented his visions.

Exit into the rose garden, then find another, less compelling room with 40 small models of his inventions. Don't waste time on the French-only video above the souvenir shop.

Your visit finishes with a stroll through the whimsical and expansive **park grounds,** with life-size models of Leonardo's inventions (including some that kids can operate), "sound stations" (in English), and translucent replicas of some of his paintings. The models and explanations make clear that much of what Leonardo observed and created was based on his intense study of nature.

## OTHER SIGHTS AND ACTIVITIES
### ▲Château Royal d'Amboise Sound-and-Light Show
On selected nights you can tour a candlelit château with music and sound effects (check dates online or at the TI). In addition, there's a summer-only theater event considered one of the best shows of its kind in the area. You'll sit on bleachers for an entertaining 90 minutes watching over 100 local volunteers from toddlers to pensioners re-create historical events. It's entirely in French, but you can rent an English audioguide. Dramatic lighting effects combine with lavish costumes, battle scenes, and fireworks to make this a most entertaining evening. Dress warmly.

**Cost and Hours:** €22 with audioguide, family deals, about 20 performances a year, 1.5-hour show runs several days per week, July 22:30-24:00, Aug 22:00-23:30, check times and prices before you go, +33 2 47 57 14 47, www.renaissance-amboise.com. Buy tickets online or from the ticket window on the ramp to the château (opens at 20:30). Seats are usually available up until the start time.

### Le Parc Mini-Châteaux
This five-acre park on the edge of Amboise (on the route to Chenonceaux) shows the major Loire châteaux in 1:25-scale models, forested with 2,000 bonsai trees. For children, it's a fun introduction to the real châteaux they'll be visiting (and there's a cool toy store). Essential English information is posted throughout the sight. You'll find other kid-oriented attractions here; consider feeding the fish in the moat (a great way to get rid of that old baguette), or take a self-driving boat for a spin.

**Cost and Hours:** Adults-€14.50, kids under 13-€10.50, daily 10:00-18:30, July-Aug from 9:30, Sept-Oct 10:30-18:00, closed Nov-early April, last entry one hour before closing, +33 2 47 23 44 57, www.parcminichateaux.com.

### Wine Tasting in Amboise
**Caveau des Vignerons** (Vins d'Amboise) is a small "cellar" offering tastings of cheeses, pâtés, and regional wines from seven differ-

LOIRE

# The Loire and Its Many Châteaux: A Historical Primer

It's hard to overstate the importance of the Loire River to France. Its place in history goes back to the very foundation of the country. As if to proclaim its storied past, the Loire is the last major wild river in France, with no dams and no regulation of its flow.

Traditional flat-bottomed boats moored along embankments are a reminder of the age before trains and trucks, when river traffic safely and efficiently transported heavy loads of stone and timber. With prevailing winds sweeping east from the Atlantic, barge tenders raised their sails and headed upriver; on the way back, boats flowed downstream with the current.

With this transportation infrastructure providing (relatively) quick access to Paris and the region's thick forests—offering plenty of timber, firewood, and excellent hunting—it's no wonder that castles were built here in the Middle Ages. The first stone fortresses went up a thousand years ago, and many of the pleasure palaces you see today rose over the ruins of those original defensive keeps.

The Hundred Years' War—roughly 1336 to 1453—was a desperate time for France. Because of a dynastic dispute, the English had a legitimate claim to the French throne, and by 1415 they controlled much of the country, including Paris. France was at a low ebb, and its king and court retreated to the Loire Valley to rule what remained of their realm. Chinon was the refuge of the dispirited king, Charles VII. He was famously visited there in 1429 by the charismatic Joan of Arc, who inspired the king to get off his duff and send the English packing.

The French kings continued to live in the Loire region for the next two centuries, having grown comfortable with their château culture. The climate was mild, hunting was good, the rivers made nice reflections, wealthy friends lived in similar luxury nearby, and the location was close enough to Paris—but still far enough away. Charles VII ruled from Chinon, Charles VIII preferred Amboise, Louis XII reigned from Blois, and François I held court in Chambord and Blois.

This was a kind of cultural Golden Age. With peace and stability, there was no need for fortifications. The most famous luxury hunting lodges, masquerading as fortresses, were built during this period—including Chenonceau, Chambord, Chaumont, Amboise, and Azay-le-Rideau. Kings (François I), writers (Rabelais), poets (Ronsard), and artists (Leonardo da Vinci) made the Loire a cultural hub. Later, these same châteaux attracted other notables, including Voltaire, Molière, and perhaps Benjamin Franklin.

Because French kings ruled effectively only by being constantly on the move among their subjects, many royal châteaux were used infrequently. The entire court (usually over 2,000 individuals)—and its trappings—had to be portable. A castle kept empty and cold 11 months of the year would suddenly become the busy center of attention when the king came to town. As you visit the castles, imagine the royal roadies setting up a kingly room—

hanging tapestries, unfolding chairs, wrestling big trunks with handles—in the hours just before the arrival of the royal entourage. The French word for furniture, *mobilier,* literally means "mobile."

When touring the châteaux, you'll notice the impact of Italian culture. From the Renaissance onward, Italian ways were fancy ways. French nobles and court ministers who traveled to Italy re-

turned inspired by the art and architecture they saw. Kings imported Italian artists and architects. It's no wonder that the ultimate French Renaissance king, François I, invited the famous Italian artist, Leonardo da Vinci, to join his court in Amboise. Tastes in food, gardens, artists, and women were all influenced by Italian culture.

Women had a big impact on Loire château life. Big personalities like kings tickled more than one tiara. Louis XV famously decorated the palace of Chenonceau with a painting of the Three Graces—featuring his three favorite mistresses.

Châteaux were generally owned by kings, their ministers, or their mistresses. A high-maintenance and powerful mistress could get her own place even when a king's romantic interest shifted. In many cases, the king or minister would be away at work or at war for years at a time—leaving home-improvement decisions to the lady of the château, who had unlimited money. That helps explain the emphasis on comfort and the feminine touch you'll enjoy while touring many of the Loire châteaux.

In 1525, François I moved to his newly built super-palace at Fontainebleau, and political power left the Loire. From then on, châteaux were mostly used as vacation rentals and hunting retreats. They became refuges for kings again during the French Wars of Religion (1562-1598)—a sticky set of squabbles over dynastic control that pitted Protestants (Huguenots) against Catholics. Its conclusion marked the end of an active royal presence on the Loire. With the French Revolution in 1789, symbols of the Old Regime, like the fabulous palaces along the Loire, were ransacked. Fast talking saved some châteaux, especially those whose owners had personal relationships with Revolutionary leaders.

Only in the 1840s were the châteaux of the Loire appreciated for their historic value. The Loire was the first place where treasures of French heritage were officially recognized and protected by the national government. In the 19th century, Romantic Age writers—such as Victor Hugo and Alexander Dumas—visited and celebrated the châteaux. Aristocrats on the Grand Tour stopped here. The Loire Valley and its historic châteaux found a place in our collective hearts and are treasured to this day.

ent vintners, with atmospheric seating inside and out (daily 10:30-19:00, closed mid-Nov-mid-March; under Château d'Amboise on Place Michel Debré, across from L'Epicerie restaurant, +33 2 47 57 23 69).

### Biking from Amboise
La Voie Royale is a 26-mile loop connecting Amboise and Chenonceaux in a roughly four-hour round-trip ride along quiet, mostly car-free paths (faster with an e-bike, get details at TI). The more direct—if less scenic—ride to Chenonceaux is about eight miles each way (allow 1.5 hours one-way) and is signed for bikes. Leading past Leonardo's Clos-Lucé, the first two miles are uphill, and the entire ride is on a road with some traffic. Serious cyclists can continue to Chaumont in 1.5 hours, connecting Amboise, Chenonceaux, and Chaumont in an all-day, 37-mile pedal.

La Route à Tours, the most appealing and level pedal from Amboise, leaves from the lower riverfront parking lot near the TI and follows the Loire downstream along a mostly dedicated bike path all the way to Tours (15 miles). You can turn your bike in there (see "Helpful Hints," earlier) and take the train back. You won't see any great castles, but the scenery is pleasant. The village of Lussault-sur-Loire makes an easy destination (2.5 miles one-way), or keep on pedaling to Montlouis, two miles past Lussault. Bike routes are shown on the "Near Amboise" map, later in this section.

## NEAR AMBOISE
### Wine Tasting in Vouvray
In the nearby town of Vouvray, 10 miles toward Tours from Amboise, you'll find wall-to-wall opportunities for wine tasting (but less impressive vineyards than in other parts of France). A majority of the vines you see are used for sparkling wines—by far the biggest sellers in Vouvray. From Amboise you can take the speedy D-952 there, or joyride on the more appealing D-1 (see the "Near Amboise" map, later in this section). Here are two top choices for testing the local sauce:

The big Cave des Producteurs de Vouvray is a smart place to start; it represents many producers, so the selection is big. You'll see its bright boutique at the first traffic signal when arriving in Vouvray on D-952 from Amboise and the east. But to taste the wine and tour the caves, continue to the next signal (at Rochecorbon) and turn right, then veer left and continue to the top, following signs to Cave de Vouvray. The staff run English-language tours of the winery and offer a good selection from the 33 producers they represent, including wines from other Loire areas (free wine tasting, 30-minute cellar tour-€4, daily 9:00-12:30 & 14:00-19:00, no midday closure July-Aug, English tour usually at about 11:30 and 16:00—call or check online to confirm times, self-guided visits also possible, 38 La Vallée Coquette in Vouvray, +33 2 47 52 75 03, www.cavedevouvray.com).

For a more intimate experience, drop by **Marc Brédif,** where you'll find a top-quality selection of Vouvray wines, excellent dessert wines, and red wines from Chinon and Bourgueil. Helpful Sarah runs the tastings (several options possible, some with nibbles). You can also tour their impressive 10th-century cellars dug into the hillside. The tour ends with a stroll past a sea of racks for hand-turning their sparkling wines (best to call or email to arrange a tasting, though drop-ins work too; €10 for cellar tour and basic tasting; Mon-Sat 10:00-12:00 & 14:30-18:00, Sun 10:00-13:00, 87 Quai de la Loire, +33 2 47 52 50 07, www.deladoucette.fr, bredif. loire@domain-bredif.fr). Coming from Amboise, you'll pass it on D-952 after Vouvray; it's tough to spot, find it on the right about 500 yards after the blue *Moncontour* signs. Park along the road, or enter at the second gate for a small lot.

# Sleeping in Amboise

Amboise is busy in the summer, but there are lots of reasonable hotels and *chambres d'hôtes* in and around the city. All hotels listed have air-conditioning unless otherwise noted.

## IN THE TOWN CENTER
**$$$$ Hôtel au Charme Rabelaisien****** is a luxurious, well-managed 10-room place. Big doors open onto a lovely courtyard with manicured gardens and a heated pool. The beautifully decorated rooms have every conceivable comfort (elevator, pay parking, 25 Rue Rabelais, +33 2 47 57 53 84, www.au-charme-rabelaisien.com, info@hotel-acr.com).

**$$$ Le Manoir les Minimes******* is a sumptuous place to experience the refined air of château life in a 17th-century mansion, with antique furniture and precious art objects in the public spaces. Its 15 large, very tasteful rooms work for those seeking luxury digs in Amboise. (Tall folks take note: Top-floor attic rooms have a lot of character but low ceilings.) Several rooms have views of Amboise's château (family rooms, closed much of winter, three blocks upriver from bridge at 34 Quai Charles Guinot, +33 2 47 30 40 40, www.manoirlesminimes.com, reservation@manoirlesminimes. com).

**$$ Hôtel le Clos d'Amboise****** is a comfortable urban refuge opening onto beautiful gardens and a small, heated swimming pool. Those with time to linger will be tempted by stay-awhile lounges, a lovely garden terrace, and traditional rooms with plush carpets (RS%, family rooms, elevator, sauna, easy and free parking, 27 Rue Rabelais, +33 2 47 30 10 20, www.leclosdamboise.com, infos@leclosamboise.com). They also offer meals at their **$$ restaurant**—best experienced on a warm night in the garden (see "Eating in Amboise," later).

**$$ Villaconcorde** hunkers below the castle with four luxurious apartments. Helpful owner Karine will check you in, and then you're on your own (no reception, etc.). These well-furnished apartments come with washers/dryers, kitchens (studios, some bigger units can sleep up to 6, 3-night minimum May-Sept, free transfer from train station possible—book ahead, 26 Rue de la Concorde, +33 6 17 25 08 42, www.villaconcorde.com, resa@villaconcorde.com).

**$$ Hôtel Bellevue\*\*\*** is a fair midrange place with 30 comfortable-enough rooms. It's centrally located on the main road, overlooking the river where the bridge hits the town. Its stylish bar/bistro has a good selection of local wines by the glass (family rooms, elevator, 12 Quai Charles Guinot, +33 2 47 57 02 26, www.hotel-bellevue-amboise.com, contact@hotel-bellevue-amboise.com).

**$ Hôtel le Chaptal\*\*** is a solid, central budget bet with smallish but tastefully designed rooms (family rooms, 11 Rue Chaptal, +33 2 47 57 14 46, www.hotel-chaptal.com, infos@hotel-chaptal-amboise.com).

**$ Hôtel le Blason\*\*** is housed in a 15th-century half-timbered building on a busy street. Run by helpful Damien and Bérangère, it has tight but comfortable and spotless rooms. Top-floor rooms have sloped ceilings and low beams but good character (quieter rooms in back, family rooms, secure pay parking, 11 Place Richelieu, +33 2 47 23 22 41, www.leblason.fr, hotel@leblason.fr).

## CHAMBRES D'HOTES

The heart of Amboise offers several solid bed-and-breakfast options.

At **$$ La Dilecta,** gentle Italian owners Andrea and Barbara rent two beautifully bright and spacious rooms in a peaceful but central home with a calming garden (6 Quai des Marais, +33 7 66 39 38 03, www.ladilecta.com, ladilecta.amboise@gmail.com).

**$ La Grange Chambres** welcomes with an intimate, flowery courtyard and four comfortable rooms, each tastefully restored with modern conveniences. There's also a common room with a fridge and tables for do-it-yourself dinners (includes breakfast, reserve with credit card but pay in cash only, where Rues Chaptal and Rabelais meet at 18 Rue Chaptal, +33 2 47 57 57 22, lagrange-amboise@orange.fr). Adorable Yveline Savin also rents a small two-room cottage and speaks fluent *franglais*.

¢ **L'Iris des Marais** is a welcoming budget B&B with three artsy and homey rooms with mini-fridges and a wild garden where you can enjoy a peaceful picnic (family rooms, includes continental breakfast, 14 Quai des Marais, +33 2 47 30 46 51, www.irisdes marais.com, vianney.frain@wanadoo.fr).

LOIRE

## NEAR THE TRAIN STATION

$ **Hôtel la Brèche,**\*\* a sleepy place near the station, has 14 fair-value rooms and a top-notch restaurant. Many of the comfortable rooms overlook the large graveled garden. While rooms on the street side are bigger, those facing the garden are quieter (excellent breakfast, easy and free parking, 15-minute walk from town center and 2-minute walk from station, 26 Rue Jules Ferry, +33 2 47 57 00 79, www.labreche-amboise.com, info@labreche-amboise.com).

## NEAR AMBOISE

The area around Amboise is peppered with accommodations of every shape, size, and price range. This region offers drivers the best chance to experience château life at affordable rates—and my recommendations justify the detour. For locations, see the "Near Amboise" map, later. Also consider the recommended accommodations in Chenonceaux.

$$$$ **Château de Pray**\*\*\*\* allows you to sleep in a 700-year-old fortified castle with hints of its medieval origins. A few minutes from Amboise, the château's 19 rooms aren't big or luxurious, but they come with character and history. The lounge is small, but the backyard terrace compensates in agreeable weather. A newer annex offers four more-modern rooms

(sleeping up to three each) with lofts, terraces, and castle views. A big pool and the restaurant's vegetable garden lie below the château (5-minute drive upriver from Amboise toward Chaumont on D-751 before the village of Chargé, Rue du Cèdre, +33 2 47 57 23 67, www.chateaudepray.fr, contact@chateaudepray.fr). The $$$$ **dining room,** cut into the hillside rock in the old *orangerie*, is a fine place to splurge (the chef has a Michelin star), but I prefer dining outside on a beautiful terrace when the weather agrees (reservations required, closed Mon-Tue).

$$$ **Château de Perreux**\*\*\* rents big rooms in a majestic 18th-century castle overlooking a huge park and meandering stream just 10 minutes by car from Amboise. Here, upscale bed-and-breakfast

service meets château-hotel ambience with 12 comfortable rooms and a pool. You'll pay more for top-floor rooms that lie under impressive wooden beams. A casual but good €35 dinner is available for guests who book ahead (family rooms, elevator, on D-1 between Nazelles and Pocé-sur-Cisse; coming from Amboise, turn left at the *Château de Perreux* sign, 36 Rue de Pocé, +33 2 47 57 27 47, www.chateaudeperreux.fr, info@chateaudeperreux.fr).

**$$$ Château des Arpentis,\*\*\*** a medieval château-hotel centrally located just minutes from Amboise, makes a classy splurge. Flanked by woods and acres of grass, and fronted by a stream and a moat, it brings you as close as you can get to château life during the Loire's golden age. Its 13 rooms are big with handsome decor—and the pool is even bigger. The place has laissez-faire management, the reception is

not staffed regularly, and there's no restaurant, but terrace-table picnics are encouraged (family rooms, elevator, +33 2 47 23 00 00, www.chateaudesarpentis.com, contact@chateaudesarpentis.com). It's on D-31 just southeast of Amboise; from the roundabout above the E. Leclerc supermarket, follow *Autrèche* signs, then look for a small sign on the right next to a tall flagpole.

**$$-$$$ Château de Nazelles Chambres\*\*\*** offers six rooms and two independent units in a 16th-century hillside manor house that comes with a cliff-sculpted pool, manicured gardens, a guest kitchen (picnics are encouraged), views over Amboise, and a classy living room with billiards. The bedrooms in the main building are traditional, while the rooms cut into the hillside come with private terraces and rock-walled bathrooms. Gentle owners Véronique and Olivier Fructus also rent a very comfortable two-room cottage with living area, kitchen, and private garden, as well as a high-end studio buried in the woods, with a sauna and Nordic bath—think hot tub (family rooms, includes breakfast, 16 Rue Tue-La-Soif, Nazelles-Négron, +33 2 47 30 53 79, www.chateau-nazelles.com, info@chateau-nazelles.com). From D-952, take D-5 into Nazelles, then turn left on D-1 and quickly veer right onto the little lane between the Town Hall and the post office (La Poste)—don't rely on GPS.

**$$ Le Moulin du Fief Gentil** is a lovely 16th-century mill house with five large and immaculate rooms set on four acres with a backyard pond (fishing possible in summer, dinner picnics anytime, fridge and microwave at your disposal), and the possibility of a home-cooked, four-course dinner with wine (includes breakfast, €34 dinner must be reserved in advance, 3 Rue de Culoison, +33

6 76 38 31 82, www.fiefgentil.com, contact@fiefgentil.com). It's located on the edge of Bléré, a 15-minute drive from Amboise and 7 minutes from Chenonceaux—from Bléré, follow signs toward *Luzillé;* it's on the right.

**$$ L'Auberge de Launay,**\*\* five miles upriver from Amboise, gets positive reviews for its easy driving access to many châteaux, fair prices, and small kitchenettes (ask for a room on the garden, 4 miles from Amboise, across the river toward Blois, 9 Rue de la Rivière in Limeray, +33 2 47 30 16 82, www.aubergedelaunay.com, info@aubergedelaunay.com). Well-prepared meals that you can re-heat are available at good prices.

# Eating in Amboise

The epicenter of the city's dining action is along Rue Victor Hugo, between Place Michel Debré and the château. While most of these restaurants are forgettable, the lively street atmosphere makes for fun dining, particularly on warm nights.

A handful of talented chefs run more intimate, less central places offering limited but top-quality selections and excellent value. Some offer just two choices for both *entrée* (starters) and *plat* (main course). Because selection and seating are limited, it's smart to check to see what's cooking, then book a day ahead.

## LIMITED-SELECTION RESTAURANTS

**$$ L'Ecluse** ("The Lockhouse") is a top choice run by friendly Arnaud. Here, you can dine outside under a weeping willow to the sound of Amboise's small stream, or stick to the sharply decorated interior. Choose between a delicious two- or three-course *menu* (no à la carte, closed Sun-Mon, book a few days ahead on weekends, a block below the château's entrance on Rue Racine, +33 2 47 79 94 91, www.ecluse-amboise.fr).

**$$ Les Arpents** has made a splash in Amboise with inventive and delicious cuisine at reasonable prices. While the decor lacks a certain warmth, the classic French cuisine is wonderful. Book ahead by a week, particularly to land a table in the courtyard (closed Sun-Mon, 5 Rue d'Orange, +33 2 36 20 92 44, https://restaurant-lesarpents.fr).

**$ La Fourchette** is Amboise's tiny family diner, with simple decor and a handful of tables inside and out. Hardworking owners make everything fresh in their open kitchen. Book ahead—the morning of the same day is fine (closed Sun and Wed, on a quiet corner near Rue Nationale at 9 Rue Malebranche, +33 6 11 78 16 98).

**$ L'Ilot** is an intimate yet convivial half-timbered place where tables gather around a central stone island and the food is old-school French heavy. *Le chef* presides over all from his island, adding a very personal touch (air-con, closed Mon-Tue, 52 Rue Rabelais, +33 2 47 57 66 58).

**$$ La Pause du Temps** is a small vintage French place, facing the town's lone traffic-free street, with carefully prepared cuisine in a charming setting (closed Mon-Tue, 80 Rue Nationale, +33 9 81 97 55 57).

**$$ L'Alliance** is a low-key place offering the kind of fresh French cuisine normally found in more formal restaurants, and it's open when most other places are closed. Here, you'll get quality ingredients prepared with an original twist, not fine decor (children's menu, good but pricey cheese tray, closed Tue, 14 Rue Joyeuse, +33 2 47 30 52 13).

## DINING ON RUE VICTOR HUGO, BELOW THE CHATEAU

These places all offer good outdoor seating.

**$ Anne de Bretagne** serves very basic café fare at cheap prices with the best view seats over Place Michel Debré (Montée Abdel-Kader, +33 2 47 57 05 46).

**$ Bigot Pâtisserie's Salon de Thé** sells luscious quiches and omelets along with delightful homemade ice cream and a terrace view. Say *bonjour* to the friendly staff, and try their specialty pastry, *puits d'amour*—"Well of Love" (Mon-Fri 9:00-19:30, Sat-Sun 8:30-20:00, where Place Michel Debré meets Rue Nationale one block off the river, +33 2 47 57 04 46).

## ELSEWHERE IN AMBOISE

Cross the bridge for the best castle views, and consider a relaxing aperitif or after-dinner drink at **$$ Le Shaker Cocktail Lounge.** It's also an ideal choice for a fun meal on a warm evening. The place is upbeat, lively, and great for kids. The very good cuisine is designed to be shared, with an appealing range of platters and *plats* (closed Sun-Mon, food served from 16:00 until late, 3 Quai François Tissard).

**$$ Hôtel le Clos d'Amboise**—one of my top recommended hotels—offers outside tables overlooking its lovely gardens as well as very comfortable and appealing seating inside. The cuisine can be first-rate and the value excellent, particularly given the lovely setting. This also makes a good choice on Sunday or Monday when many other places are closed—or if you just want an intimate and peaceful evening (daily, for details, see "Sleeping in Amboise," earlier).

**$ L'Ancrée des Artistes** is a reliable, centrally located *crêperie*. This young-at-heart place has music to dine by and easygoing servers (three-course crêpe *menus,* good meat dishes grilled on stones—called *pierres*, and casserole-like *cocottes*, daily July-Aug, off-season closed Sun evening and Mon, 35 Rue Nationale, +33 2 47 23 18 11).

$$$ **Hôtel la Brèche** is a deservedly trendy place for foodies, with excellent service and gourmet cuisine at manageable prices (€44, €56, and €72 *menus*). Choose between the pleasing dining room and the large garden when weather permits. Stretch your legs and cross the river to the restaurant (closed Sun-Mon; for details, see "Sleeping in Amboise," earlier).

## NEAR AMBOISE

For an elegant castle dining experience with a Michelin star, consider making the quick drive to **Château de Pray** if you can get a spot on the terrace (call ahead; for details, see "Sleeping in Amboise," earlier).

# Amboise Connections

## By Bus

Buses leave for **Chenonceaux** once or twice daily (Mon-Sat only—none on Sun, 25 minutes, departs Amboise about 9:50, returns from Chenonceaux at about 12:25, allowing you about 1.5 hours at the château during its most crowded time; in summer, there's also an afternoon departure at about 15:00 with a return from Chenonceaux at about 17:50; confirm times with the TI or www.remi-centrevaldeloire.fr). The Amboise stop (direction: Chenonceaux)—called Théâtre—is between Place St-Denis and the river on the west side of Avenue des Martyrs de la Résistance, across from the Théâtre de Beaumarchais; in Chenonceaux, the bus stops across the street from the TI (a 5-minute walk to the château entrance). For more flexibility, consider taking a train back instead (see page 43).

Buses also run to **Tours** and are cheaper but slower than trains (8/day Mon-Sat, none on Sun).

## By Taxi

A taxi from Amboise to Chenonceau costs about €30 (€43 on Sun and after 19:00, €7 pickup fee, call +33 2 47 57 13 53, +33 6 12 92 70 46, +33 2 47 57 30 39, or +33 6 88 02 44 10).

## By Train

*To Loire Châteaux*: **Chenonceaux** (6/day, 45-60 minutes, transfer at St-Pierre-des-Corps—check connections and return times to avoid long waits), **Blois** (14/day, 20 minutes), **Chaumont** (14/day, 10 minutes to Onzain on the Amboise-Blois route, then 30-minute walk or 10-minute bus, 8/day), **Tours** (12/day, 25 minutes, allows

LOIRE

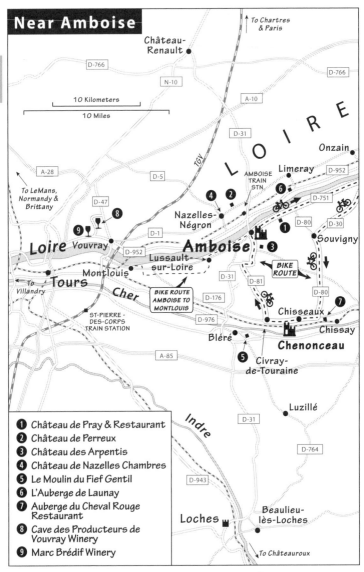

**Near Amboise**

To Chartres & Paris

Château-Renault

D-766

N-10

A-10

D-766

10 Kilometers

10 Miles

D-31

L O I R E

Onzain

D-5

TGV

AMBOISE TRAIN STN.

Limeray

D-952

A-28

To LeMans, Normandy & Brittany

D-47

❹ ❷

Nazelles-Négron

❻

D-751

D-30

❽

D-1

❶

D-80

Souvigny

❾

Vouvray

Loire

D-952

Amboise · ❸

BIKE ROUTE

Lussault-sur-Loire

Montlouis

To Villandry

Tours

Cher

BIKE ROUTE AMBOISE TO MONTLOUIS

ST-PIERRE-DES-CORPS TRAIN STATION

D-31

D-81

D-176

D-976

Bléré

Chisseaux

❼

D-80

Chissay

Chenonceau

A-85

❺

Civray-de-Touraine

Luzillé

Indre

D-31

D-764

D-943

❶ Château de Pray & Restaurant
❷ Château de Perreux
❸ Château des Arpentis
❹ Château de Nazelles Chambres
❺ Le Moulin du Fief Gentil
❻ L'Auberge de Launay
❼ Auberge du Cheval Rouge Restaurant
❽ Cave des Producteurs de Vouvray Winery
❾ Marc Brédif Winery

Beaulieu-lès-Loches

Loches

To Châteauroux

connections to châteaux west of Tours), **Chinon** (7/day, 2 hours, transfer in Tours), and **Azay-le-Rideau** (6/day, 1.5 hours, transfer in Tours).

*To Destinations Beyond the Loire:* Frequent trains link Amboise to the regional train hub of St-Pierre-des-Corps in suburban Tours (20/day, 15 minutes). There you'll find reasonable connections to distant points (including the TGV to Paris' Gare Montparnasse).

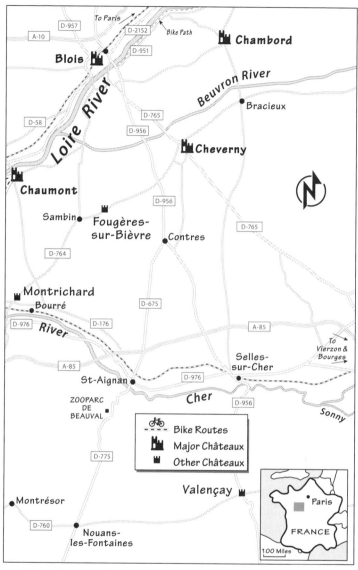

Transferring in Paris can be the fastest way to reach many French destinations, even in the south.

From Amboise you can catch the train to: **Paris Gare Montparnasse** (10/day, 1.5 hours with change to TGV at St-Pierre-des-Corps, requires TGV reservation), **Paris Gare d'Austerlitz** (3/day direct, 2 hours, no reservation required, more with transfer), **Sarlat-la-Canéda** (3/day, 6 hours, change at St-Pierre-des-Corps, then TGV to Bordeaux, then train through Bordeaux vineyards to Sarlat), **Limoges** (10/day, 4 hours, 1-2 transfers, near Oradour-sur-Glane, requires bus from Limoges), **Mont St-Michel** (5/day, 5.5 hours with several transfers), **Bayeux** (4/day, 5 hours, best requires transfers at St-Pierre-des-Corps and Caen, skip those with transfer in Paris as they require a station change), **Beaune** (6/day, 6 hours, transfers at Nevers and/or St-Pierre-des-Corps; more with multiple connections and reservations), **Bourges** (roughly hourly—though fewer midday, 2-3 hours, change at St-Pierre-des-Corps).

## By Minivan Excursion

Most of these companies run shared tours (and private tours by request) that depart from TIs in Amboise or Tours. While on the road, you may get a running commentary—but you're on your own at the sights (discounted châteaux tickets available from the driver allow you to skip ticket lines). Reserve a week ahead by email, or two to three days by phone. Day-trippers from Paris find these services convenient.

**Acco-Dispo** runs half- and all-day English tours from Amboise with live commentary while driving to all the major châteaux six days a week (Mon-Sat). Costs vary with the itinerary (half-day tours-€42/person, full-day-€66/person; groups of 2-8 people, +33 6 82 00 64 51, www.accodispo-tours.com, contact@accodispo.com). Acco-Dispo also runs multiday tours of the Loire and Brittany.

**Touraine Evasion** runs half-day tours daily with recorded narration from Amboise to Chambord and Chenonceau (€42/person) and all-day tours that add Cheverny (€66/person). They also have many château options out of Tours (daily in-season, none in winter, +33 6 07 39 13 31, www.tourevasion.com).

**Loire Valley Tours** offers all-day itineraries from Amboise and Tours with guided tours of châteaux and sights. These upscale tours include admissions, lunch, and wine tasting (about €200/person, +33 2 47 79 40 20, www.loire-valley-tours.com, contact@loire-valley-tours.com).

**A la Française Tours** runs similar itineraries to Loire Valley Tours, but with a younger vibe. They also offer half-day tours from €79/person (tours depart from Amboise or Tours TI, +33 2 46 65 51 57, www.alafrancaise.fr, contact@alafrancaise.fr).

# Chenonceau

Château de Chenonceau is the toast of the Loire and worth ▲▲▲. This 16th-century Renaissance palace arches gracefully over the Cher River and is impeccably maintained, with fresh flower arrangements in the summer and roaring log fires in the winter. This château is wonderfully organized for visitors, but it's also one of the most-visited châteaux in France—so carefully follow my crowd-beating tips.

While Chenonceau is the name of the château, and Chenonceaux is the name of the town, they're pronounced the same: shuh-nohn-soh. The town itself—a one-road village with well-priced hotels and some fine eating options—makes a good home base for drivers (see recommendations later, under "Town of Chenonceaux").

**Tourist Information:** The ignored TI is on the main road from Amboise as you enter the village (July-Aug daily 9:30-19:00, closed at lunchtime on Sun; Sept-June Mon-Sat 9:30-13:00 & 14:00-18:00—until 17:00 in winter, closed Sun; +33 2 47 23 94 45).

## GETTING THERE

From Amboise, you can get here by **train** (6/day, 45-60 minutes), or faster, by **bus,** which drops off at the TI (1-2/day, Mon-Sat only, none on Sun, 25 minutes—see page 33 for details on this bus). There are also frequent train connections from Tours. The unstaffed train station sits between the village and the château.

Minivan **excursions** from Amboise and Tours are also available (see "By Minivan Excursion" under "Amboise Connections" on page 36).

You can also take a **taxi** from Amboise (€30 one-way, €43 on Sun and after 19:00, €7 pickup fee; for contact info, see "Taxi" under "Helpful Hints" for Amboise on page 17).

If **driving,** plan on a 20-minute walk from the parking lot to the château. Don't leave any valuables visible in your car.

## ORIENTATION TO CHATEAU DE CHENONCEAU

**Cost and Hours:** €15, less for kids under 18, advance tickets highly recommended in summer and on holiday weekends; daily 9:00-19:00, closes earlier off-season. The château's gardens stay open later on selected evenings in most seasons, with music to enjoy as you stroll. While not worth planning your trip around, it's a pleasant experience.

**Information:** +33 2 47 23 90 07, www.chenonceau.com.

**Timed Entry for the Château:** Because spaces are tight inside the château, a reserved time slot is required to enter. Smart travelers plan around Chenonceau's crowds by buying a ticket in advance online—when you purchase your ticket, you'll select an entry time. You can enter and enjoy the grounds any time on the day of your visit.

**Without an Advance Ticket:** This place gets slammed in high season. If you arrive *sans* reservation, come early (by 9:00) or late (after 17:00). Otherwise, during the busiest times, you may not be able to get same-day entry to the château. Avoid slow lines by purchasing your ticket from the machines just inside the ticket office (US credit cards work, but instructions in English are hit-or-miss—withdraw your card at the prompt *"retirez"*).

**Tours:** The interior is fascinating—but only if you take advantage of the excellent 20-page **booklet** (included with entry) or rent the wonderful **multimedia guide** (€4). Pay for the guide when buying your ticket (before entering the château grounds), then pick it up just inside the château's door.

**Services:** WCs are available by the ticket office and behind the old stables.

**Eating:** A reasonable **$$** cafeteria is next door to the hospital room. Fancy **$$$** meals are served in the *orangerie* behind the stables (Restaurant l'Orangerie). There's a cheap *crêperie/*sandwich shop at the entrance gate. While picnics are not allowed on the grounds, there are picnic tables in a park near the parking lot.

**River Fun:** Paddling under the Château de Chenonceau is a memorable experience. In good weather the château has rental **rowboats** (€7/30 minutes, July-Aug daily 10:00-19:00, 4 people/boat). **Canoe Company** offers rentals and shuttles on the Cher River (€12-25/person depending on how far you go, +33 6 70 13 30 61, www.canoe-company.fr).

## BACKGROUND

Enter the grounds and walk 15 level minutes to the castle. Find a riverside view to get oriented. Although earlier châteaux were built for defensive purposes, Chenonceau was the first great pleasure palace. Nicknamed the "château of the ladies," it housed many famous women over the centuries. The original owner, Thomas Bohier, was away on the king's business so much that his wife, Katherine Briçonnet, made most of the design decisions during construction of the main château (1513-1521).

In 1547, King Henry II gave the château to his mistress, Diane de Poitiers, who added an arched bridge across the river to access the hunting grounds. She enjoyed her lovely retreat until Henry II died (pierced in a jousting tournament in Paris); his vengeful wife, Catherine de' Medici, unceremoniously kicked Diane out (and into the château of Chaumont, described later). Catherine added the three-story structure on Diane's bridge. She died before completing her vision of a matching château on the far side of the river, but

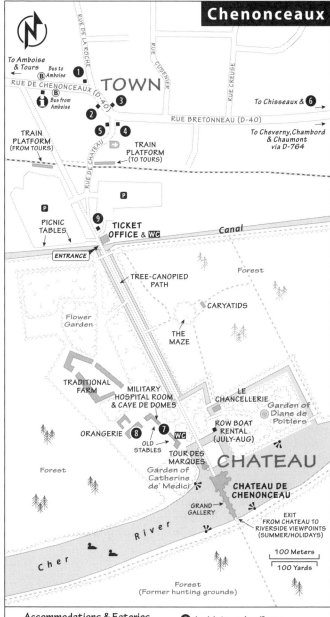

# Chenonceaux

**TOWN**

RUE DE LA ROCHE

RUE CUBENIER

RUE CREUSE

To Amboise & Tours

Bus to Amboise

RUE DE CHENONCEAUX (D-40)

Bus from Amboise

RUE DE CHENONCEAUX (D-40)

RUE BRETONNEAU (D-40)

To Chisseaux &

To Cheverny, Chambord & Chaumont via D-764

TRAIN PLATFORM (FROM TOURS)

TRAIN PLATFORM (TO TOURS)

RUE DE CHATEAU

PICNIC TABLES

TICKET OFFICE & WC

Canal

ENTRANCE

TREE-CANOPIED PATH

Forest

CARYATIDS

Flower Garden

THE MAZE

TRADITIONAL FARM

MILITARY HOSPITAL ROOM & CAVE DE DOMES

LE CHANCELLERIE

Garden of Diane de Poitiers

ROW BOAT RENTAL (JULY-AUG)

ORANGERIE

OLD STABLES

WC

TOUR DES MARQUES

CHATEAU

Garden of Catherine de' Medici

CHATEAU DE CHENONCEAU

Forest

GRAND GALLERY

EXIT FROM CHATEAU TO RIVERSIDE VIEWPOINTS (SUMMER/HOLIDAYS)

Cher River

100 Meters

100 Yards

Forest (Former hunting grounds)

## Accommodations & Eateries

❶ Auberge du Bon Laboureur
❷ Hôtel la Roseraie
❸ Relais Chenonceaux
❹ Hostel du Roy
❺ La Maison des Pages
❻ To Auberge du Cheval Rouge
❼ Cafeteria
❽ Restaurant l'Orangerie
❾ Crêperie & Ticket Machines

not before turning Chenonceau into *the* place to see and be seen by the local aristocracy. (Whenever you see a split coat of arms, it belongs to a woman—half her husband's and half her father's.)

## VISITING THE CHATEAU

Strutting like an aristocrat down the tree-canopied path to the château, you'll cross three moats and two bridges, and pass the Tour des Marques, an old round tower that predates the main building. (There's a fun plant maze partway up on the left, and beyond that, four monumental caryatids that used to be on the facade of the chateau.) Notice the tower's fine limestone veneer, added so the top would better fit the new château.

The main château's original **oak door** greets you with the coats of arms of the first owners. The knocker is high enough to be used by visitors on horseback. The smaller door within the large one could be for two purposes: to slip in after curfew, or to enter during winter without letting out all the heat.

Once inside, you'll tour the château in a mostly clockwise direction. Take time to appreciate the beautiful brick floor tiles, lavishly decorated ceilings, and elegant hallways. As you continue, follow your pamphlet or multimedia guide, and pay attention to these details (that don't include all rooms you'll see):

In the **guard room,** the best-surviving tiles from the original 16th-century floor are near the walls—imagine the entire room covered with these faience tiles. And though the tapestries kept the room cozy, they also functioned to tell news or recent history (to the king's liking, of course). The French-style joist beams feature Catherine de' Medici's monogram. You'll see many more tapestries and monograms in this château.

The superbly detailed **chapel,** with its original 1521 wood gallery above the entry, survived the vandalism of the Revolution because the fast-thinking lady of the palace filled it with firewood. Angry masses were supplied with mallets and instructions to smash everything royal or religious. While this room was both, all they saw was stacked wood. The hatch door provided a quick path to the kitchen and an escape boat downstairs. The windows, blown out during World War II, are replacements from the 1950s. Look for graffiti in English left behind by the guards who protected Mary, Queen of Scots (who stayed here after her marriage to King François II).

The centerpiece of the **bedroom of Diane de Poitiers** is, ironically, a severe portrait of her rival, Catherine de' Medici, at 40 years old. Notice the various monograms in the room. You've already seen Catherine's Chanel-like double-C insignia. Henri II flaunts his singular H. And combining the two seems to form mirrored Ds...perhaps showing Henri's preference for his mistress Diane.

The 16th-century tapestries are among the finest in France. Each one took an average of 60 worker-years to make. Study the complex compositions of the *Triumph of Charity* (over the bed) and the violent *Triumph of Force*.

At 200 feet long, the three-story **Grand Gallery** spans the river. The upper stories house double-decker ballrooms and a small museum. Notice how differently the slate and limestone of the checkered floor wear after 500 years. Imagine grand banquets here. Catherine, a contemporary of Queen Elizabeth I of England, wanted to rule with style. She threw wild parties and employed her ladies to circulate and soak up all the political gossip possible from the well-lubricated Kennedys and Rockefellers of her realm. Parties included grand fireworks displays and mock naval battles on the river. The niches once held statues—Louis XIV took a liking to them, and they now decorate the palace at Versailles.

In summer and during holidays, you can take a quick walk outside for more good palace **views:** Cross the bridge, pick up a re-entry ticket, then stroll the other bank of the Cher (across the river from the château). During World War I, the Grand Gallery served as a military hospital, where more than 2,200 soldiers were cared for—picture hundreds of beds lining the gallery. And in World War II, the river you crossed marked the border between the collaborationist Vichy government and Nazi-controlled France. Back then, Chenonceau witnessed many prisoner swaps, and at night, château staff would help resistance fighters and Jews cross in secret. Because the gallery was considered a river crossing, the Germans had their artillery aimed at Chenonceau, ready to destroy the "bridge" to block any Allied advance.

Double back through the gallery to find the sensational state-of-the-art (in the 16th century) **kitchen** below. It was built near water (to fight the inevitable kitchen fires) and in the basement; because heat rises, it helped heat the palace. Cross the small bridge (watch your head) to find the stove and landing bay for goods to be ferried in and out.

From here, find **François I's drawing room** (a.k.a. Muse/Three Graces Room), with a painting featuring King Louis XV's three favorite mistresses, then visit the King Louis XIV Room, with an over-the-top framed painting of Louis (who appreciated Chenonceau).

Back on the main floor, the staircase leading **upstairs** wowed royal guests. It was the first nonspiral staircase they'd seen...quite a treat in the 16th century. When open, the balcony provides views of the gardens, which originally supplied vegetables and herbs. (Diane built the one to the right; Catherine, the prettier one to your left.) The estate is still full of wild boar and deer—the primary dishes of past centuries. You'll see more lavish bedrooms on this floor. Small

LOIRE

side rooms may show fascinating old architectural sketches of the château. The walls, 20 feet thick, were honeycombed with the flues of 224 fireplaces and passages for servants to do their pleasure-providing work unseen. There was no need for plumbing: Servants fetched, carried, and dumped everything.

Above the Grand Gallery is the **Medici Gallery,** now a mini museum for the château. Displays in French and English cover the lives of six women who made their mark on Chenonceau (one of them had a young Jean-Jacques Rousseau, who would later become an influential philosopher, as her personal secretary). There's also a timeline of the top 10 events in the history of the château and a cabinet of curiosities.

Go to the **top floor** to peek inside the somber bedchamber and mourning room of Louise de Lorraine, widow of Henri III. Stabbed by a renegade Dominican monk, the king dictated this message for his wife on his deathbed: "My dear, I hope that I shall bear myself well. Pray to God for me and do not move from there." Louise took him literally and spent the last 11 years of her life in meditation and prayer at Chenonceau. Perpetually dressed in the then-traditional mourning color, she became known as the White Queen. Take a close look at the silver teardrops that adorn the black walls before paying homage at the 16th-century portrait of Henri III.

Escape the hordes by touring the **two gardens** with their post-card-perfect views of the château. The upstream garden of Diane de Poitiers hasn't changed since she first commissioned it in 1547. Designed in the austere Italian style, the water fountain was revolutionary in its time for its forceful jet. The downstream garden of Catherine de' Medici is more relaxed, with tree roses and lavender gracing its lines in high season.

**Military Hospital Room and Traditional Farm:** These sights are best seen after you've toured the château and gardens. The military hospital room (with effective English explanations) is located in the château stables and gives an idea of what the Grand Gallery was like when it housed wounded soldiers during World War I. You can taste the owner's wines in the atmospheric **Cave des Dômes** below. Just past the stables you can stroll around a traditional farm. Imagine the production needed to sustain the château while making your way through the vegetable and flower gardens toward the exit.

## TOWN OF CHENONCEAUX

This one-road, sleepy village makes a good home base for drivers and a workable base for train travelers who don't mind connections.

**Sleeping:** Hotels are a good value in Chenonceaux, and there's one for every budget. You'll find them *tous ensemble* on Rue du Dr. Bretonneau, all with free and secure parking.

**$$$ Auberge du Bon Laboureur\*\*\*\*** turns heads with its ivied facade, lush terraces, and stylish indoor lounges and bars. The staff is a tad stiff, but you still get gorgeous four-star rooms with every comfort at three-star prices (family rooms and suites, air-con, heated pool, fine gardens, finer restaurant, 6 Rue du Dr. Bretonneau, +33 2 47 23 90 02, www.bonlaboureur.com, contact@bonlaboureur.com).

**$$ Hôtel la Roseraie\*\*\*** has good "bones" and 22 comfortable rooms at fair prices, but the place could use a face-lift (air-con, pool, restaurant—pass on their dinner, closed mid-Nov-March, 7 Rue du Dr. Bretonneau, +33 2 47 23 90 09, www.hotel-chenonceau.com, laroseraie-chenonceaux@orange.fr).

**$ Relais Chenonceaux\*\*** greets guests with a nice patio and a mix of rooms. The best rooms are in the annex; those in the main building are plain and above a restaurant, but inexpensive (family rooms, +33 2 47 23 98 11, 10 Rue du Dr. Bretonneau, www.chenonceaux.com, info@chenonceaux.com).

**$ Hostel du Roy\*\*** offers 30 spartan but well-priced rooms, some around a garden courtyard, and a mediocre but cheap restaurant. Hardworking Nathalie runs the place with panache (family rooms, 9 Rue du Dr. Bretonneau, +33 2 47 23 90 17, www.hostelduroy.com, hostelduroy@wanadoo.fr).

**Eating:** Pickings are slim for good dining here. **$$$ Auberge du Bon Laboureur** restaurant (*menus* from €58) is a fine splurge for a country elegant experience; otherwise it's basic fare, unless you're willing to drive about a mile to Chisseaux and book ahead a day or so for the *très* traditional **$$ Auberge du Cheval Rouge.** Here you'll enjoy fine cuisine at affordable prices, either inside a pretty dining room or on a verdant patio (closed Mon-Wed, 30 Rue Nationale, Chisseaux, +33 2 47 23 86 67, www.auberge-duchevalrouge.com).

**La Maison des Pages** has some bakery items, sandwiches, cold drinks to go, and just enough groceries for a modest picnic (closed Wed and Sun, on the main drag between Hostel du Roy and Hôtel la Roseraie).

**Connections:** It's easy to connect Chenonceaux by train to **Tours,** though beware of big afternoon gaps in the schedule (10/day, 30 minutes; trains to Tours depart from the château side of

LOIRE

the tracks), with connections to **Chinon, Azay-le-Rideau,** and **Langeais.** To reach **Amboise,** you can either take the train (6/day, 1 hour, transfer at St-Pierre-des-Corps) or bus (1-2/day, Mon-Sat only, none on Sun, 25 minutes, departs Chenonceaux at about 12:25, in summer also at about 17:50, catch bus across the street from the TI, www.remi-centrevaldeloire.fr).

# Blois

Bustling Blois (pronounced "blwah") feels like the Big Apple after all of those rural villages and castles. Blois owns a rich history,

dolled-up pedestrian areas, and a darn impressive château smack in its center. With convenient access to Paris, Blois makes a handy base for train travelers (though accommodation options are limited); Chambord and Cheverny are within reach by excursion bus (cheap, high season only) or taxi (which also serve Chaumont). Frequent train service to Paris and Amboise enables easy stopovers in Blois.

From this once-powerful city, the medieval counts of Blois governed their vast lands and vied with the king of France for dominance. The center of France moved from Amboise to Blois in 1498, when Louis XII inherited the throne (after Charles VIII had his unfortunate head-banging incident in Amboise). The château you see today is living proof of this town's 15 minutes of fame. But there's more to humble Blois than just its château. Visit the flying-buttressed St. Nicolas Church, find the medieval warren of lanes and lovely rose garden below St. Louis Cathedral, and relax in a café on Place Louis XII.

## Orientation to Blois

Unlike most other Loire châteaux, Blois' Château Royal sits smack in the city center, with no forest, pond, moat, or river to call its own. It's an easy walk from the train station, near ample underground parking, and just above the TI. Below the château, Place Louis XII marks the hub of traffic-free Blois, with cafés and shops lining its perimeter. Rue du Commerce, leading up from the river, is Blois' primary shopping street. Atmospheric cafés and restaurants hide in the medieval tangle of lanes below St. Louis Cathedral and around St. Nicolas Church. Blois was heavily bombed in World War II, leaving much of the old town in ruins, but the château survived.

Today, the city largely ignores its river and celebrates Saturdays with a lively market (until about 13:00) centered on Place Louis XII. Sundays are awfully quiet in Blois.

## ARRIVAL IN BLOIS

**Train** travelers can walk 10 minutes straight out of the station downhill on Avenue du Dr. Jean Laigret to the TI and château (follow *Château* signs), or take a two-minute taxi from in front of the station.

**Drivers** follow *Centre-Ville* and *Château* signs (metered parking along Avenue du Dr. Jean Laigret or inside at Parking du Château—first 30 minutes free, then about €2/2 hours).

## TOURIST INFORMATION

The TI is below the château entrance, just off Place du Château at 5 Rue de la Voûte du Château (see the "Blois" map). They sell discounted tickets when purchased for several châteaux (Mon-Sat 9:00-13:00 & 14:00-19:00, Sun until 13:00; Oct-March Mon-Sat 10:00-13:00 & 14:00-17:00, closed Sun; +33 2 54 90 41 41, www.bloischambord.com). To explore the center of Blois, buy the TI's walking-tour map (€2, free with their app, red and purple routes are best), or follow my suggested walking route under "Other Sights and Activities," later. The TI has schedules for the Navette-Châteaux bus, other bus services, and Eco Shuttle minivan excursions to Chambord and Cheverny (see "Blois Connections," later). They also have information on bike rentals and bike paths.

## HELPFUL HINTS

**Baggage Storage:** You have several good choices for bag storage in Blois. **Détours de Loire** can store large suitcases for €5/bag (free if you rent a bike—see next listing). The recommended **Hôtel Anne de Bretagne** will also store bags for a small fee. You can store smaller bags at the **TI** (small fee) and in the château's free **lockers** with paid admission. Remember to reclaim your bag before they close.

**Bike Rental: Détours de Loire** bike rental/bag storage is a block below the train station at 39 Avenue du Dr. Jean Laigret (daily April-Sept, +33 2 54 56 07 73, https://detoursdeloire.com).

**Car Rental: Avis, Hertz, and Europcar** are all present in Blois but a long walk from the train station (consider a cab).

**Launderette:** A self-service launderette is at 6 Rue St-Lubin (daily 7:00-21:00).

**Local Guide: Fabrice Maret** lives in Blois and is a skilled teacher (see page 10 for details).

LOIRE

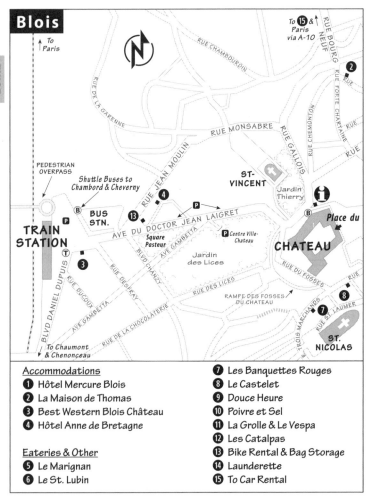

**Blois**

To Paris

RUE CHAMBOURDIN

To ⓯ & ↑ Paris via A-10

RUE BOURG NEUF

❷

RUE FORTE CHARTAINE

RUE DE LA GARENNE

RUE MONSABRE

RUE GALLOIS

RUE CHEMONTON

RUE JEAN MOULIN

ST-VINCENT

Jardin Thierry

ℹ️

PEDESTRIAN OVERPASS

Shuttle Buses to Chambord & Cheverny

RUE DU DOCTOR JEAN LAIGRET

🅿

Ⓑ

Place du

ⓑ BUS STN.

❹

🅿 Centre Ville-Chateau

TRAIN STATION

🅿

⓭

AVE DU DOCTOR JEAN LAIGRET

Square Pasteur

AVE GAMBETTA

CHATEAU

🅣

❸

BLVD CHANZY

Jardin des Lices

RUE DU FOSSES

BLVD DANIEL DUPUIS

RUE DUCOUX

RUE DESFRAY

RUE DES LICES

RAMPE DES FOSSES DU CHATEAU

RUE TROIS MARCHANDS

❽

AVE GAMBETTA

RUE DE LA CHOCOLATERIE

❼

RUE ST. LAUMER

To Chaumont & Chenonceau

ST. NICOLAS

**Accommodations**
- ❶ Hôtel Mercure Blois
- ❷ La Maison de Thomas
- ❸ Best Western Blois Château
- ❹ Hôtel Anne de Bretagne

**Eateries & Other**
- ❺ Le Marignan
- ❻ Le St. Lubin

- ❼ Les Banquettes Rouges
- ❽ Le Castelet
- ❾ Douce Heure
- ❿ Poivre et Sel
- ⓫ La Grolle & Le Vespa
- ⓬ Les Catalpas
- ⓭ Bike Rental & Bag Storage
- ⓮ Launderette
- ⓯ To Car Rental

# Sights in Blois

## ▲▲CHATEAU ROYAL DE BLOIS

Size up the château from the big square before entering. A castle has inhabited this site since the 900s. Even though parts of the building date from the Middle Ages, notice the complete absence of defensive towers, drawbridges, and other fortifications. Gardens once extended behind the château and up the hill to a forest (where the train station is today). A walk around the building's perimeter (to the right as you face it) reveals more of its beautiful Renaissance facade.

Kings Louis XII and François I built most of the château you

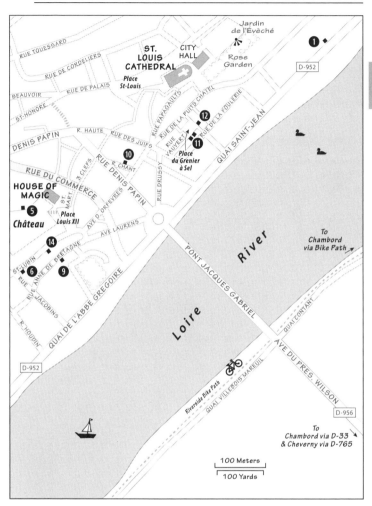

see today, each calling it home during their reigns. That's Louis looking good on his horse in the niche. The section on the far right looks like a church but was actually the château's most important meeting room (more on this later).

**Cost and Hours:** €13, €6.50 for kids under 18, €20 combo-ticket with House of Magic or sound-and-light show, €28 covers all three, daily 9:00-18:30, Nov-March until 17:00.

**Information:** +33 2 54 90 33 33, www.chateaudeblois.fr.

**Sound-and-Light Show:** This 45-minute "show" takes place in the center courtyard and features projections with a historical narrative of the château (€11, covered by château combo-tickets, free headset provides English translation, daily mid-April-Sept at about 22:00).

**Tours:** At the ticket office, pick up the helpful brochure, then read the well-presented displays in each room. The snazzy Histo-Pad tablet with images and sound is free, but the less-techy audioguide is €3 (go figure).

**Visiting the Château:** Begin in the **courtyard,** where four wings—ranging from Gothic to Neoclassical—underscore this château's importance over many centuries. Stand with your back to the entry to get oriented. The medieval parts of the château are the brick-patterned sections (to your left and behind you), both built by Louis XII. While work was under way on Chambord, François I (who apparently was addicted to home renovation) added the elaborate Renaissance wing (to your right; early 16th century), centered on a protruding spiral staircase and slathered with his emblematic salamanders. Gaston d'Orléans inherited the place in the 1600s and wanted to do away with the messy mismatched styles. He demolished a church that stood across from you (the chapel to your left is

all that remains) and replaced it with the clean-lined, Neoclassical structure you see today. Luckily, that's as far as he got.

Visit the interior clockwise, and focus on the Renaissance wing. Start across the courtyard in the Neoclassical wing (not worth a long look), and climb up to the plush **royal apartments of François I** in the Renaissance wing. Immerse yourself in richly tiled, ornately decorated rooms with some original furnishings (excellent explanations posted). You'll see busts and portraits of some of the château's most famous residents (including portraits from François' lineage several rooms down). Enter the stunning **Queen's Room,** where Catherine de' Medici died, and learn about the dastardly 1588 murder of the duke of Guise, which took place in these apartments. In the late 1500s, the devastating Wars of Religion pitted Protestant against Catholic and took a huge toll on this politically and religiously divided city—including the powerful Guise brothers. King Henry III (Catherine de' Medici's son)

had the devoutly Catholic duke assassinated to keep him off the throne.

Walk downstairs to the small **lapidary museum** with an engaging display of statues and architectural fragments from the original château (love the gargoyles). There's also a good

LOIRE

exhibit on the history of the castle with models of its construction at various phases.

Continue on to the dazzling **Hall of the Estates-General.** This is the oldest surviving part of the château (predating Louis and François), where the Estates-General met twice to deliberate who would inherit the throne from Henry III, who had no male heir. (You've already learned how Henry resolved that question.)

End your visit with a walk through the small **fine-arts museum.** Located just over the château's entry, this 16th-century who's-who portrait gallery lets you put faces to the characters that made this château's history.

## OTHER SIGHTS AND ACTIVITIES

### House of Magic (Maison de la Magie)

The home of Jean-Eugène Robert-Houdin, the illusionist whose name was adopted by Harry Houdini, offers a fun history of illusion and magic. Kids enjoy the gift shop, the shows, and the interactive displays (the good English brochure helps you navigate). Several daily 30-minute shows have no words, so they work in any language. Magicians roam the place pulling rabbits out of hats. A fun dragon snorts his stuff on the outside of the building on the half-hour.

**Cost and Hours:** €11, €6.50 for kids under 18, covered by château combo-tickets described earlier; daily 10:00-12:30 & 14:00-18:30, magic "séance" schedule posted at entry—or check the website (likely roughly every hour). Located at the opposite end of the square from the château, +33 2 54 90 33 33, www.maisondelamagie.fr.

### A Walk Through Blois' Historic Center

There's little to do along the river except to cross Pont Jacques Gabriel for views back to the city. But Blois' old town is worth a ramble. Although much of the historic center was destroyed by WWII bombs, it has been rebuilt with traffic-free streets and pleasing squares.

For a taste of medieval Blois, drop down the steps below the House of Magic and turn right into Place Louis XII, ground zero in the old city; from here, walk down Rue St-Lubin (after a few blocks it turns into Rue des Trois Marchands). Follow along as the street curves to the left and continue until you see the church of **St. Nicolas.** The towering church, with its flying buttresses, dates from the late 1100s and is worth a peek inside for its beautifully lit apse and its blend of Gothic and Romanesque styles. Find Rue Anne de Bretagne skirting left and behind the church and track it back to Place Louis XII. From here, pedestrian-friendly streets like Rue St-Martin lead north to Rue du Commerce, the town's main shopping drag, and to peaceful medieval lanes below Blois' other hill, crowned by **St. Louis Cathedral.** Finish your walk with a steep climb up from cute Place du Grenier à Sel to the rose garden that sits just below the cathedral and City Hall (Hôtel de Ville). The esplanade above the rose garden offers rooftop views over the city.

### Biking from Blois

Blois is well positioned as a starting point for biking forays into the countryside. Cycling from Blois to Chambord is a level, 1.5-hour, one-way ride along a well-marked, 13-mile route, much of it an elaborate bike-only lane that follows the river's left (eastern) bank. You can loop back to Blois without repeating the same route and connect to a good network of other bike paths (the TI's free *Les Châteaux à Vélo* map shows area bike routes). You can also take a 26-mile one-way ride to Amboise, stopping at garden-rich Chaumont-sur-Loire on the way, then return to Blois by train with your bike (lugging a heavy e-bike on the train is a challenge). For bike rental, see "Helpful Hints" for Blois, earlier.

## Sleeping in Blois

Blois has a scarcity of worthwhile hotels.

**$$$ Hôtel Mercure Blois\*\*\*\*** is modern and made for businesspeople, but it's reliable, with big, superior two-level rooms and a riverfront location a 15-minute walk below the château (air-con, elevator, pay parking, 28 Quai Saint-Jean, +33 2 54 56 66 66, https://all.accor.com).

**$$ La Maison de Thomas** is a mod B&B that doubles as a wine-tasting boutique specializing in Loire vintages. It's an old building, but all five rooms have been updated with Euro-chic decor (includes breakfast, cash only, uphill from the château near the pedestrian main drag at 12 Rue Beauvoir, ask for directions to street parking, +33 9 81 84 44 59, www.lamaisondethomas.fr, resa@lamaisondethomas.fr, Guillaume).

**$$ Best Western Blois Château\*\*\*** has stylish decor, small-but-sharp rooms, all the comforts you'd expect from this chain, and is ideally located for train travelers (air-con, elevator, across from the train station at 8 Avenue du Dr. Jean Laigret, +33 2 54 56 85 10, www.bestwestern.fr, hotelbloisgare.fr@gmail.com).

**$ Hôtel Anne de Bretagne\*\*** is a welcoming place, offering a solid two-star value with 29 well-appointed rooms (with good fans but no air-con), a central location near the château and train station, and a welcoming terrace. Ask for a room on the quiet side of the building facing the terrace. They also rent bikes—best to book in advance (family rooms, no elevator, 150 yards uphill from Parking du Château, 5-minute walk below the train station at 31 Avenue du Dr. Jean Laigret, +33 2 54 78 05 38, www.hotelannedebretagne. com, contact@hotelannedebretagne.com).

# Eating in Blois

If you're stopping in Blois around lunchtime, plan on eating at one of the places in the lower part of town. **Le Marignan,** on the square in front of the château, works for a drink to watch the stately mansion opposite the château becoming the "dragon house," as monsters crane their long necks out its many windows on the half-hour.

Diners can start their evening with a drink at the popular watering hole **Le St. Lubin,** a café-bar (closed Sun, 16 Rue St-Lubin).

## BETWEEN THE CHATEAU AND THE RIVER

The traffic-free streets between the château and the river are home to many cafés with standard, easy meals.

**$$ Les Banquettes Rouges,** a block above St. Nicolas Church's left transept, is your best bet for foodie pleasures. It features fine regional dishes with creative twists—try the duck or pan-fried veal liver. You'll dine in a red booth—as the name suggests (closed Sun-Mon, reservations smart, 16 Rue des Trois Marchands, +33 2 54 78 74 92, www.lesbanquettesrouges.com).

**$ Le Castelet,** also near St. Nicolas, is simple and cheap with decent vegetarian choices (closed Sun and Wed, 40 Rue St-Lubin, +33 2 54 74 66 09).

**$$ Douce Heure** is a cheery *salon gourmand* on Place Louis XII's southwest corner. The extensive menu of homemade beverages includes iced teas, traditional hot chocolate, and fruit cocktails—the strawberry, raspberry, and rose are excellent (good salads, quiches, and wraps; great desserts, Tue-Sun 12:00-19:00, closed Mon, 4 Rue Anne de Bretagne).

## ELSEWHERE IN BLOIS

**$$ Poivre et Sel,** just a few blocks from the Pont Jacques, offers new takes on traditional French cuisine in a faux-rustic setting. Dine on the ground floor or in the open loft. Weekend reservations are recommended (12:00-14:00 & 19:00-22:00, closed Sun and Wed, 9 Rue du Chant des Oiseaux, +33 2 54 78 07 78).

**Between the Cathedral and the River:** To dine cheaply on an atmospheric square with few tourists in sight, find Place du Grenier à Sel (a block from the river, below St. Louis Cathedral) and consider these places: **$$ La Grolle** specializes in *savoyard* cuisine with fondues, raclettes, *tartiflette,* and other melted-cheese dishes, with lighter options available in summer (closed Sun-Mon, 5 Rue Vauvert, +33 2 36 23 64 65). Next door, **$$ Le Vespa** does a basic

Franco-Italian mix, including pizzas (pleasant interior seating, closed Sun-Mon except in summer, 11 Rue Vauvert, +33 2 54 78 44 97).

Save room for dessert and try the crêpes and good salads at the friendly **$ Les Catalpas** (daily for lunch and dinner, 1 Rue du Grenier à Sel, +33 2 54 56 86 86).

# Blois Connections

## By Bus

You can get to the châteaux of Chambord and Cheverny cheaply by bus in any season, but it's not simple. Get current schedules online or from the TI. Chaumont is accessible by train and then bus.

The **Navette-Châteaux bus,** with trips to **Chambord, Cheverny,** and (skippable) **Beauregard** (daily July-Sept, runs less often Easter-June and Oct-early Nov, no service early Nov-Easter). It departs from Blois station at approximately 9:15, 11:30, and 13:45 (check for possible differences on Sat). Buses stop first at Chambord, then Cheverny, and finally at Beauregard. There are three return trips to Blois—verify times at a TI or online at www. remi-centrevaldeloire.fr—click "Tourisme" (€3 bus fare, discounts offered on châteaux entries including the Château Royal in Blois; buy tickets from TI or bus driver).

On days when the Navette-Châteaux is not running, **lines 2 and 4** provide a similar but more limited service to Chambord or Cheverny (get details at the website listed above or at the TI).

These buses all originate at the train station parking lot. For the Navette-Châteaux bus, turn left out of the station door and keep left to find the second bus shelter. You can also board these buses at the stop below and behind the Blois château (3 minutes later than the train station departure).

## By Minivan Excursion

**Eco Shuttle** offers daily excursions to surrounding châteaux at good rates, leaving from the Blois train station and from Place du Château by the TI. Look for excursions to Chambord (€25/person) or Chambord and Cheverny (€39). Book ahead at the TI or online (+33 6 49 26 34 35, www.ecoshuttle41.com).

## By Taxi

Blois taxis wait in front of the station and offer excursion fares to

Chambord, Chaumont, or Cheverny (about €36 one-way from Blois to any of these three châteaux, €110 round-trip to Chambord and Cheverny, €160 for Chambord and Chenonceau, much more expensive on Sun, 8-person minivans available, +33 2 54 78 07 65). These rates are per cab, making the per-person price downright reasonable for groups of three or four.

## By Train

From Blois to: Amboise (14/day, 20 minutes), Tours (hourly, 40 minutes), Chaumont (14/day, 10-minute train, then 30-minute walk to château or 10-minute bus transfer; info under Chaumont description, later), Chinon (6/day, 2.5 hours, transfer in Tours and possibly in St-Pierre-des-Corps), Azay-le-Rideau (6/day, 2 hours, transfer in Tours and possibly in St-Pierre-des-Corps), Paris Austerlitz (about hourly, 2.5 hours with transfer in St-Pierre-des-Corps or Orléans); Paris Montparnasse (12/day, 2 hours with change in St-Pierre-des-Corps).

# Chambord

With its huge scale and prickly silhouette, Château de Chambord, worth ▲▲▲, is the granddaddy of the Loire châteaux. It's surrounded by Europe's largest enclosed forest park, a game preserve defined by a 20-mile-long wall and teeming with wild deer and boar. Chambord (shahm-bor) began as a simple hunting lodge for bored Blois counts and became a monument to the royal sport and duty of hunting. (Hunting was considered important to keep the animal population under control and the vital forests healthy.)

The château's massive architecture is the star attraction—particularly the mind-boggling double-helix staircase. Six times the size of your average Loire castle, the château has 440 rooms and a fireplace for every day of the year. The château is laid out as a keep in the shape of a Greek cross, with four towers and two wings surrounded by stables. Its four floors are each separated by 46 stairs, creating sky-high ceilings. The ground floor has reception rooms, the first floor up has the royal apartments, the second floor houses temporary exhibits and a hunting museum, and the rooftop offers a viewing terrace to plot your next hunting adventure. Special exhibits describing Chambord at key moments in its history help animate the place. Because hunters could see best after autumn leaves fell, Chambord was a winter palace (which helps explain the 365 fireplaces). Only 80 of Chambord's rooms are open to the public—but that's plenty.

Because the château is so big, crowded rooms are not an issue. It helps that there's no one-way, mandatory tour route—you're free to roam like a duke surveying his domain.

## GETTING THERE

**Without a car** from Blois, you have several options (see "Blois Connections," earlier). Buses drop you (and pick up) in the P-1 bus parking lot, 100 yards from the information center and "village." It's a level 1.5-hour bike ride from Blois to Chambord (see "Biking from Blois," earlier). Minivan excursions also run from Amboise (see page 36).

**With a car,** allow 25 minutes to drive from Blois, 45 minutes from Amboise, 55 minutes from Chenonceaux, and 15 minutes from Cheverny. You'll pay €6 to park (pay at machines near the lots when you arrive to avoid end-of-day lines, credit cards only).

## ORIENTATION TO CHATEAU DE CHAMBORD

**Cost and Hours:** €14.50, daily 9:00-18:00, Oct-March until 17:00. The primary ticket office is at the information center in Chambord's "village" (a cluster of shops and services) near the main parking area, but you can also get tickets inside the château.

**Information:** +33 2 54 50 40 00, www.chambord.org.

**Tours:** This château requires helpful information to make it come alive. The free handout is useful, and most rooms have enough explanations. For a lot more context, rent the €6.50 HistoPad tablet guide at the château. Or take a guided tour in English (€5, generally daily mid-June-Sept at 11:15).

**Services:** The big information center is located in a flashy building near the closest parking area to the château. Nearby you'll also find a cluster of shops and services, including souvenir shops, a wine-tasting room, and several choices for a quick meal. There's a WC behind the primary ticket office and another at the château itself. The bookshop inside the château has a good selection of children's books.

**Eating:** There are three convenient locations for finding a bite to eat: in the village (near the information center—many choices, from crêpes to three-course meals), a snack stand sitting alone as you approach the château (quieter, with best château view—salads, sandwiches, and ice cream), and inside the château courtyard (with a good selection at fair prices).

**Cruising the Grounds:** A network of leafy lanes crisscrosses the vast expanse contained within the 20-mile-long wall. Explore

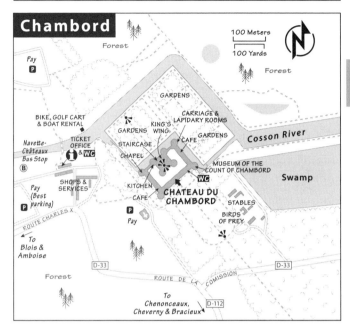

the park on a bike (€7/hour), a 4-person pedalcart (€20/hour), or a golf cart (€28/45 minutes, 2-4 people). Your roaming area is more restricted in the golf cart, but you'll cover lots more ground than on foot. You can also rent electric boats (€22/30 minutes—which is plenty) and cruise the château-front canal. Bikes, boats, and carts are all rented on the canal across the small bridge near the village.

**Gardens:** The original Renaissance gardens behind the château can be accessed with a château entry ticket. The best views of the gardens are from the château's rooftop terrace.

**Horse and Bird of Prey Show:** The 60-minute show is not worth most people's time or money (€15.50, less for kids or with château combo-ticket, mid-July-Aug daily in morning and afternoon except no Mon show, fewer off-season, reserve ahead, reservations@chambord.org).

**Views:** The best view of the château depends on the light. Walk out of the back of the château into the gardens for fine views, or walk straight out the main entrance a few hundred yards for exquisite looks back to the château. Near the village, cross the canal and turn right for more exceptional views. From wherever you view the château, imagine its cupolas covered in royal blue with gold trim.

**Night Lights:** The château is bathed in ever-changing colors after dark.

LOIRE

## BACKGROUND

Starting in 1518, a young François I created this "weekend retreat," employing 1,800 workmen for 15 years. (You'll see his signature salamander symbol everywhere.) François I was an absolute monarch—with an emphasis on absolute. In 32 years of rule (1515-1547), he never once called the Estates-General to session (a rudimentary parliament in *ancien régime* France). This imposing hunting palace was another way to show off his power. Countless guests, like Charles V—the Holy Roman Emperor and most powerful man of the age—were invited to this pleasure palace of French kings...and were totally wowed.

The grand architectural plan of the château—modeled after an Italian church—feels designed as a place to worship royalty. Each floor of the main structure is essentially the same: Four equal arms of a Greek cross branch off a monumental staircase, which leads up to a cupola. From a practical point of view, the design pushed the usable areas to the four corners. This castle, built while the pope was erecting a new St. Peter's Basilica, is like a secular rival to the Vatican.

Construction started the year Leonardo died, 1519. The architect is unknown, but an eerie Leonardo-esque spirit resides here. The symmetry, balance, and classical proportions combine to reflect a harmonious Renaissance vision that could have been inspired by Leonardo's notebooks.

Typical of royal châteaux, this palace of François I was rarely used. Because any effective king had to be on the road to exercise his power, royal palaces sat empty most of the time. In the 1600s, Louis XIV renovated Chambord, but he visited it only six times (for about two weeks each visit). And while the place was ransacked during the Revolution, the greatest harm to Chambord came later, from neglect.

## VISITING THE CHATEAU

I've covered the highlights, floor by floor.

**Ground Floor:** This stark level shows off the general plan—four wings, small doors to help heated rooms stay warm, and a massive staircase. In a room just inside the front door, on the left, you can watch a worthwhile, 18-minute video—look for a screen on the side wall with English subtitles.

The attention-grabbing **double-helix staircase** dominates the open vestibules and invites visitors to climb up. Its two spirals are interwoven, so people can climb up and down and never meet. Find the helpful explanation of the staircase posted on the wall. Walk to the center of the stairway and gaze up, then enjoy fine views of the vestibule action, or just marvel at the playful Renaissance capitals carved into its light tuff stone. Don't leave this floor without making a quick stop to see the kitchens in the far-left corner (detailed explanations posted); imagine the challenge of feeding 440 rooms of guests.

**First Floor Up:** Here you'll find the most interesting rooms. Starting in the rooms opposite a big ceramic stove (added in the 18th century), tour this floor basically clockwise. You'll enter the lavish apartments in the **king's wing** and pass through the grand bedrooms of Louis XIV, his wife Maria Theresa, and, at the far end after the queen's boudoir, François I (follow *l'Aile Royale* signs, staying inside the gallery). These theatrical bedrooms place the royal beds on raised platforms—getting them ready for some nighttime drama. The furniture in François' bedroom was designed so it could be easily disassembled and moved with him.

Return to the grand stairway via the outside walkways and find the seven-room **Museum of the Count of Chambord** (Musée du Comte de Chambord). The last of the French Bourbons, Henri d'Artois (a.k.a. the count of Chambord) was next in line to be king when France decided it didn't need one. He was raring to rule—you'll see his coronation outfits, throne, and even souvenirs from the coronation that never happened. Learn about the man who believed he should have become King Henry V but who lived in exile from the age of 10. Although he opened the palace to the public and saved it from neglect, he actually visited this château only once, in 1871.

The **chapel,** tucked off in a side wing, is interesting only for how unimpressive and remotely located it is. It's dwarfed by the mass of this imposing château—clearly designed to trumpet the glories not of God, but of the king of France.

**Second Floor:** Beneath beautiful coffered ceilings (notice the "F" for François and hundreds of salamanders) is a series of ballrooms that once hosted post-hunt parties. From here, you'll climb up to the rooftop, but first lean to the center of the staircase and look down its spiral.

**Rooftop:** A pincushion of spires and chimneys decorates the rooftop viewing terrace. From a distance, the roof—with its frilly forest of stone towers—gives the massive château a deceptive lightness. From here, ladies could scan the estate grounds, enjoying the spectacle of their ego-pumping men out hunting. On hunt day, a line of beaters would fan out and work inward from the distant walls, flushing wild game to the center, where the king and his buddies waited. The showy lantern tower of the tallest spire glowed with a nighttime torch when the king was in.

Gaze up at the grandiose tip-top of the tallest tower, capped with the king's fleur-de-lis symbol. It's a royal lily—not a cross—that caps this monument to the power of the French king.

Duck into the rooftop room that holds an intriguing exhibit

about Chambord during World War II, and learn how this huge place was used as a warehouse for storing precious art from the Louvre. Find the copy of *Mona Lisa* ready for packing.

**Renaissance Gardens:** Back on the ground floor, walk out the central rear door to explore the Renaissance gardens mixed with modern sculptures, and enjoy good views back to the château.

**In the Courtyard:** In the far-right corner as you face the château, next to the café, a door leads to the Rolls-Royce of **carriage rooms** and the fascinating **lapidary rooms.** Here you'll come face-to-face with original stonework from the roof, including the graceful lantern cupola, with the original palace-capping fleur-de-lis. Imagine having to hoist that load. The volcanic tuff stone used to build the spires was soft and easy to work, but not very durable—particularly when so exposed to the elements. Several displays explain the ongoing renovations to François' stately pleasure dome.

# Cheverny

This stately hunting palace, a ▲▲ sight, is one of the more lavishly furnished Loire châteaux. Because the immaculately preserved Château de Cheverny (shuh-vehr-nee) was built and decorated in a relatively short 30 years, from 1604 to 1634, it has a unique architectural harmony and unity of style. From the start, this château has been in the Hurault family, and Hurault pride shows in its flawless preservation and intimate feel (it was opened to the public in 1922).

The charming viscount and his family still live on the third floor (not open to the public, but you'll see some family photos). Cheverny was spared by the French Revolution; the count's relatives were popular then, as today, even among the village farmers.

## GETTING THERE

You can reach Cheverny by bus or minivan excursion from Blois (see "Blois Connections" on page 52), or by minivan excursion from Amboise or Tours (see page 36). The bus stop is across from the château entry, by the church. Drivers can park for free at the château.

**LOIRE**

## ORIENTATION TO CHATEAU DE CHEVERNY

**Cost and Hours:** €13.50, €18 combo-ticket includes Tintin "adventure" rooms, daily 9:15-18:30, Nov-March 10:00-17:00; +33 2 54 79 96 29, www.chateau-cheverny.fr.

**Hunting Dogs:** The château's 100 hunting dogs are a worthwhile sight as they await their next hunt or meal. The famous public feeding of the dogs was stopped during the Covid-19 pandemic, and there is no plan to resume. But nothing (other than buildings) is ever set in stone here, so check the website in case they reverse their decision.

**Eating and Sleeping:** The château sits alongside a pleasant village, with a small grocery store and cafés offering good lunch options (the town also has a few hotels).

## VISITING THE CHATEAU

As you walk across the manicured grounds toward the gleaming château, the sound of hungry hounds may follow you. Lined up across the facade are sculpted medallions with portraits of Roman emperors, including Julius Caesar (above the others in the center). As you enter the château, pick up the excellent self-guided tour brochure, which describes the interior beautifully.

Your visit starts in the lavish **dining room,** decorated with leather walls and a sumptuous ceiling. Next, as you climb the stairs to the private apartments, look out the window and spot the *orangerie* across the gardens. It was here that the *Mona Lisa* was hidden (along with other treasures from the Louvre) during World War II.

On the first floor, turn right from the stairs and tour the I-could-live-here **family apartments** with silky bedrooms, kids' rooms, and an intimate dining room. On the other side of this floor is the impressive **arms room** with weapons, a sedan chair, and a snare drum from the count of Chambord. The **king's bedchamber** is literally fit for a king. Study the fun ceiling art, especially the "boys will be boys" cupids.

On the top floor, peek inside the **chapel** before backtracking down to the ground floor. Browse the left wing and find a family tree going back to 1490, a grandfather clock with a second hand that's been ticking for 250 years, and a letter of thanks from George Washington to this family for their help in booting out the English.

Leaving the château, consider a short stroll through the gardens to the *orangerie,* which today houses a kids' play area and a garden café.

## OTHER SIGHTS AT THE CHATEAU

### Dog Kennel

Barking dogs remind visitors that the viscount still loves to hunt (he goes twice a week year-round). The kennel (200 yards in front of the château, look for *Chenil* signs) is home to 100 dogs—half English foxhound and half French Poitou, bred to have big feet and bigger stamina. They're given food once a day (two pounds each in winter, half that in summer). The trainer knows every dog's name—how he can tell them apart is a mystery to me.

### More Château Sights

Near the kennel, **Tintin** comic lovers can enter a series of fun rooms designed to take them into a Tintin "adventure" (called *Les Secrets de Moulinsart*—it's in French, ask for English translations); hunters can inspect an antler-filled **trophy room;** and gardeners can prowl the château's fine **kitchen gardens** (free, behind the dog kennel).

Gardens: Cheverny's huge park is open to the public. The tulips are gorgeous when blooming, as are the fruit trees. Ask what's blooming, then consult your brochure.

### Wine Tastings at the Château Gate

Opposite the entry to the château sits a slick wine-tasting room, **La Maison des Vins.** It's run by an association of 32 local vintners. Their mission: to boost the reputation of Cheverny wine (which is fruity, light, dry, and aromatic compared to the heavier, oaky wines made farther downstream). For most, the best approach is to enjoy four free tastes from featured bottles of the day, offered with helpful guidance (€6-11 bottles). Wine aficionados can pay to sample among the 96 bottles by using modern automated dispensers (3 wines-€4, 7 wines-€6.50). Even if just enjoying the free tasting, wander among the spouts. Each gives the specs of that wine in English (daily 11:00-13:15 & 14:15-18:00, open during lunch July-Aug, closed in winter, +33 2 54 79 25 16, www.maisondesvinsdecheverny.fr).

# Chaumont-sur-Loire

A castle has been located on this spot since the 11th century; the current version is a ▲▲ sight (▲▲▲ for garden or horse lovers). The first priority at Chaumont (show-mon) was defense; the second, it seems, was gardening. Gardeners will appreciate the elaborate Festival of Gardens that unfolds next to the château every year, and modern-art lovers will enjoy how works have been incorporated into the gardens, château, and stables. If it's cold, you'll also appreciate that the château is heated in winter (rare in this region).

## GETTING THERE

The train between Blois and Amboise can drop you (and your bike) in Onzain, a 30-minute roadside walk—or 10-minute shuttle bus or taxi ride—across the river to the château (14 trains/day, 10 minutes from Amboise or Blois; 8 buses/day, https://bus.azalys.agglopolys.fr, hover over "Horaires," then click on "Domaine de Chaumont-sur-Loire Shuttle"; train and shuttle bus-€4, bus only-€1.25). It's a €14 taxi ride to the château (call +33 6 04 15 89 02 or email contact@taxi-seillac.fr).

Other options include biking (Chaumont is about 11 level miles from Amboise or Blois) or taxi (about €36 from Amboise center or Blois train station).

To avoid the hike up, drivers should skip the river-level entrance (closed in winter) and park up top behind the château (open all year). From the river, drive up behind the château (direction: Montrichard); at the first roundabout follow signs to *Château* and *Festival des Jardins*.

## ORIENTATION TO DOMAINE DE CHAUMONT-SUR-LOIRE

**Cost and Hours:** €19 combo-ticket covers château, stables, and Festival of Gardens; €14 off-season combo-ticket covers château and stables (gardens closed); open daily mid-April-Sept 10:00-19:30, Oct-mid-Nov until 18:00, mid-Nov-mid-April until 17:00, last entry 45 minutes before closing.

**Information:** +33 2 54 20 99 22, www.domaine-chaumont.fr.

**Tours:** A superb English handout and excellent posted explanations in each room make the €4 multimedia guide unnecessary.

**Festival of Gardens:** This annual exhibit, with 25 elaborate gardens arranged around a different theme each year, draws rave reviews from international gardeners. It's as impressive as the Chelsea Flower Show in England, but without the crowds—if you love contemporary garden design, you'll love this. When the festival is on (from about the third week in April till early November), you'll find several little cafés and reasonable lunch options scattered about the hamlet. Chaumont also hosts a winter garden festival inside several greenhouses.

**Yard Art:** The château, outbuildings, horse stables, and park are peppered with modern-art installations year-round. The grounds around the château are meticulously maintained and lovely in any season.

## BACKGROUND

The Chaumont château you see today was built mostly in the 15th and 16th centuries. Catherine de' Medici forced Diane de Poitiers to swap Chenonceau for Chaumont; you'll see tidbits about both women inside.

There's a special connection to America here. Jacques-Donatien Le Ray, a rich financier who owned Chaumont in the 18th century, was a champion of the American Revolution. He used his wealth to finance loans in the early days of the new republic (and even let Benjamin Franklin use one of his homes in Paris rent-free for nine years). Unfortunately, the US never repaid the loans in full and eventually Le Ray went bankrupt.

Ironically, the American connection saved Chaumont during the French Revolution. Le Ray's son emigrated to New York and became an American citizen, but returned to France when his father deeded the castle to him. During the Revolution, he was able to turn back the crowds set on destroying Chaumont by declaring that he was now an American—and that all Americans were believers in *liberté, égalité,* and *fraternité.*

Today's château offers a good look at a top defense design from the 1500s: on a cliff with a dry moat, big and small drawbridges with classic ramparts, loopholes for archers, and handy holes through which to dump hot oil on attackers.

## VISITING THE CHATEAU

Your walk through the palace—restored mostly in the 19th century—is described by the flier you'll pick up when you enter. As the château has more rooms than period furniture, your tour is splashed with modern-art exhibits that fill otherwise empty spaces. The first "period" rooms you'll visit (in the east wing) show the château as it appeared in the 15th and 16th centuries. Your visit ends in the west wing, which features furnishings from the 19th-century owners.

The castle's medieval **entry** is littered on the outside with various coats of arms. As you enter, take a close look at the two drawbridges and the wall-embedded hooks that held them up (a new mechanism allows the main bridge to be opened with the touch of a button). Once inside, the heavy defensive feel is replaced with palatial luxury. Peek into the courtyard—during the more stable mid-1700s, the fourth wing, which had enclosed the courtyard, was taken down to give the terrace its river-valley view. The château kitchens are down the steps from the entry, though there's little of interest to see unless you enjoy wild art installations.

Entering the château, signs direct you along a one-way loop path *(suite de la visite)* through the château's boutique, starting up a stone spiral stairway.

Catherine de' Medici, who missed her native Florence, brought a touch of Italy to all her châteaux, and her astrologer (Ruggieri) was so important that he had his own (plush) room—next to hers. You'll see **Ruggieri's bedroom** first and a portrait of him. **Catherine's bedroom** has a 16th-century throne—look for unicorns holding a shield. The Renaissance-style bed is a reproduction from the 19th century. The fascinating collection of medallions in the cases date from 1772, when Le Ray invited the Italian sculptor Jean-Baptiste Nini to work for him. Find the case with medallions of ceramic portrait busts depicting Benjamin Franklin, Marie Antoinette, Voltaire, and Catherine the Great. Peer into the chapel below before leaving Catherine's room.

The exquisitely tiled **Salle de Conseil** has a grand fireplace and elaborate tapestries designed to keep this conference room warm. The treasury box in the **guard room** is a fine example of 1600s-era locksmithing. The lord's wealth could be locked up here as safely as possible in those days, with a false keyhole, no handles, and even an extra-secure box inside for diamonds.

A spiral staircase leads up through many unfurnished rooms and galleries of contemporary art. Instead, head downstairs to find rooms decorated in 19th-century style. The **dining room's** fanciful limestone fireplace is exquisitely carved. Find the food (frog legs, snails, goats for cheese) across the front, spot the maid with the bellows on the left, and look up high for the sculptor with a hammer and chisel. Your visit ends with a stroll through the 19th-century library, the billiards room, and the living room. The porcupines over the fireplace and elsewhere are thanks to the Duke of Orléans, who adopted the porcupine as his emblem in 1394.

In the **courtyard,** study the entertaining spouts and decor on the walls, and remember that this space was originally enclosed on all sides. Chaumont has one of the best château views of the Loire River—rivaling Amboise for its panoramic tranquility.

Veer right, leaving the château to find the **stables** *(écuries),* which were entirely rebuilt in the 1880s. The medallion above the gate reads *pour l'avenir* (for the future), which demonstrates an impressive commitment to horse technology. Despite the advent of steam engines, horses remained for a time the most important means of moving people and supplies.

Inside, circle clockwise—you can almost hear the clip-clop of horses walking. Notice the deluxe horse stalls, padded with bins and bowls for hay, oats, and water, complete with a strategically placed drainage gutter. The horse kitchen *(cuisine des chevaux)* produced mash twice weekly for the horses, which were named for

Greek gods and great châteaux. You'll also see an impressive display of riding harnesses, saddles, and several carriages parked and ready to go.

The **estate** is set in a 19th-century landscape, with woodlands and a fine lawn. More English than French, it has rolling open terrain, follies such as a water tower, and a designer *potager* (vegetable garden) with an imaginative mix of edible and decorative plants. Its trees were imported from throughout the Mediterranean world to be enjoyed—and to fend off any erosion on this strategic bluff.

# West of Tours

Several worthwhile sights gather in the area west of Tours, including Azay-le-Rideau, Langeais, Villandry, Rivau, Ussé, and the Abbaye Royale de Fontevraud. The appealing towns of Chinon and smaller Azay-le-Rideau make good home bases for seeing these sights. Trains provide access to many châteaux (via Tours) but are time-consuming; you're better off with your own car or a minivan excursion—these depart only from Tours or Amboise (see "Chinon Connections," later, and "Amboise Connections," earlier). The Tours TI, at the train station (20 minutes by train from Chinon), offers the best variety of minivan excursions for this area (+33 2 47 70 37 37, www.tours-tourisme.fr).

Here's a good way for drivers to organize their day: Start at Azay-le-Rideau, and continue to Villandry (15-minute drive). If you've had enough châteaux for the day, skip the fortress at Langeais (10-minute drive), but consider visiting the charming village, which is central to two good routes to Chinon or the Abbey of Fontevraud (each about 40 minutes). One option takes you through the vineyards along D-35 through Bourgueil (tastings recommended later). The other option takes you across the bridge at Langeais and follows D-16 west, passing through the riverside village of Bréhémont to Ile St-Martin. (Along the way, a left turn to Rigné-Ussé brings you to a superb view of that castle). Chinon and the Abbey of Fontevraud are each about 20 minutes from Rigné-Ussé.

# Chinon

This pleasing, sleepy town straddles the Vienne River and hides its ancient streets under a historic royal fortress. Henry II (Henry Plantagenet of England), Eleanor of Aquitaine, Richard the Lionheart, and Joan of Arc all called this town home for a while. Today's Chinon (shee-nohn) is best known for its popular red wines and enjoys a fraction of the visitors that Amboise does.

# Orientation to Chinon

Chinon stretches out along the Vienne River, and everything of
interest to travelers lies between it and the hilltop fortress. Charming Place du Général de Gaulle—ideal for café-lingering—is in
the center of town. Rue Rabelais is Chinon's traffic-free shopping
street, with restaurants, bars, and cafés—and is as lively as it gets
in peaceful Chinon.

## TOURIST INFORMATION

The **main TI** is by the river in the town center, a 15-minute walk
from the train station. You'll find discounted châteaux tickets, wine-
tasting and bike-rental information, and an English-language brochure with a basic self-guided town walk that's much longer than
it needs to be (TI open daily 9:30-13:00 & 14:00-18:00, no lunch
break July-Aug, shorter hours and closed Sun off-season, 1 Rue
Rabelais, +33 2 47 93 17 85, www.azay-chinon-valdeloire.com). A
**TI annex** is located near the fortress entrance on Rue Porte du
Château (daily July-Aug 10:00–13:00 & 14:00–18:00).

## HELPFUL HINTS

**Market Days:** A bustling market takes place all day Thursday
(food in the morning only) on Place Jeanne d'Arc (east end of
town). There's also a sweet little market on Saturday and Sunday mornings, around Place du Général de Gaulle.

**Laundry: Salon Lavoir** is near the bridge at 40 Quai Charles VII
(daily 7:00-21:00).

**Bike and Canoe Rental: Clan Canoë Kayak & Vélo** is on the
river, next to the campground (bikes-€17/day; canoes-€17/2
hours or €20/half-day, includes shuttle; €23-39 to combine
bike and canoe in a half/full day; cash only, closed off-season,
Quai Danton, +33 6 23 82 96 33, https://chinon-canoe.fr). For
more on biking and canoeing, see "Other Chinon Activities,"
later.

**Taxi:** Call +33 2 47 50 70 50 or mobile +33 6 50 97 87 30.

**Car Rental:** It's best to rent at the St-Pierre-des-Corps train station.

**Parking:** You'll find metered but cheap parking in town. Or park
for free at the fortress (castle) and take the elevator down to
the town.

**Traditional Riverboat Cruise:** Two-hour rides on flat-bottom
boats are possible from March to October at 15:30, but verify
with TI (€19, www.bateaux-promenades-chinon.com, next to
bike/canoe rental described earlier).

**Best Views:** Chinon's best views are from the fortress. You'll also find
terrific rooftop and river views below the fortress along Rue du

Coteau St-Martin, and rewarding river views to Chinon from the bridge in the center of town—or, even better, by crossing the bridge and turning right (small riverfront café May-Sept). Return to the bridge after dinner for a fine night view.

# Chinon Walk

Chinon offers a peaceful world of quiet cobbled lanes, a handful of historic buildings, and few tourists. Follow this self-guided walk and read plaques at key buildings to learn more about this city's historic importance.

• *Begin this short walk from the highest point of the bridge that crosses the Vienne River, and enjoy the great view (which is even better after dark).*

**Chinon Riverbank:** Chinon is sandwiched between the Vienne River (which flows into the Loire River only a few miles from here) and an abrupt cliff. People have lived along the banks of this river since prehistoric times. The Gallo-Romans built the first defenses in Chinon 1,600 years ago, and there's been a castle up on that hill for more than a thousand years—which pretty much predates every other castle you'll visit in the Loire area. The castle walls are extensive: That skinny, rounded clock tower on the right actually sits in the middle of the castle and was a key entrance to the fortress during the Middle Ages. Starting in 1044, the fortress-castle became an important outpost for the king of France, and by 1150 Henry II Plantagenet (king of England) made this the center of his continental empire. A few hundred years later, Charles VII took refuge behind those walls during the Hundred Years' War, during which Chinon was France's capital city.

Down on the water, you'll see reproductions of the traditional wooden boats once used to shuttle merchandise up and down the river; some boats ventured as far west as the Atlantic.

• *Walk toward the city, then make a right along the riverbank and find the big statue that honors a famous Renaissance writer and satirist.*

**Rabelais Statue:** The great French writer François Rabelais was born here in 1494. You'll see many references to him in his proud hometown. His best-known work, *Gargantua and Pantagruel,* describes the amusing adventures of father-and-son giants and was set in Chinon. Rabelais' vivid humor and savage wit are, for many, quintessentially French—there's even a French word for it: *rabelaisien.* In his bawdy tales, Rabelais critiqued society in ways that deflected outright censorship—though the Sorbonne called his work obscene. Also a monk and a doctor, Rabelais is considered the first great French novelist, and his farces were a voice against the power of the Church and the king.

• *Turn your back on Rabelais and follow the cobbled sidewalk leading to the center of Chinon's main square.*

**Place du Général de Gaulle:** The town wall once sat on the wide swath of land running from this square down to the river, effectively walling the city off from the water. This explains why, even now, Chinon seems to turn its back on its river. In medieval times, the market was here, just outside the wall. The Town Hall (Hôtel de Ville) building, originally an arcaded market, was renovated only in the 19th century. Today it flies three flags: Europe, France, and Chinon (with its three castles).

• *Turn left down...*

**Rue Voltaire:** If the old wall still stood, you'd be entering town through the east gate. Walk along a strip of 16th-, 17th-, and 18th-century houses to find a trio of fun wine-tasting possibilities. A half-block to the right is the funky little **Musée Animé du Vin,** at the next corner is the laid-back **Cave Voltaire wine shop,** and a right turn on the next small lane leads to **Caves Painctes** and the quarry where the stone for the castle originated (all covered later, under "Sights in Chinon").

• *Continue a few blocks farther down Rue Voltaire into the historic city center.*

**Old Town:** In the immediate post-WWII years, there was little money or energy to care for beautiful old towns. But in the 1960s, new laws and sensitivities kicked in, and old quarters like this were fixed up and preserved. Study the local architecture. **La Maison Rouge** (at #38) is a fine example of the town's medieval structures: a stone foundation and timber frame, filled in with whatever was handy—in this case, red bricks. With dense populations crowding within the protective town walls, buildings swelled wider at the top to avoid blocking congested streets. **La Maison Bleue** next door shows slate siding and looks like it belongs in Normandy. The plaque tells us that Joan of Arc dismounted her horse at this spot in 1429.

Pop into the ancient **bookshop** on the corner. I asked the owner where he got his old prints. He responded, "Did you ever enjoy a friend's mushrooms and ask him where he found them? Did he tell you?"

The **town museum** (Musée Le Carroi) is across the street. Its plaque recalls that this building housed an Estates-General meeting, convened by Charles VII, in 1428. Just around the corner, find a good tower view (and a public WC).

• *From here the street changes names to Rue Haute St-Maurice. You can continue in the same direction and find the Caves Plouzeau wine cellars at #94 (described later). If you'd rather visit the castle, hike up Rue Jeanne d'Arc (or take the elevator—see below) to the fortress.*

LOIRE

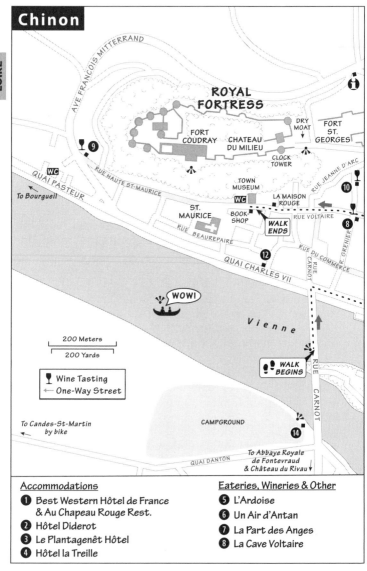

**Chinon**

ROYAL FORTRESS

DRY MOAT
FORT ST. GEORGES
FORT COUDRAY
CHATEAU DU MILIEU
CLOCK TOWER
RUE JEANNE D'ARC

WC
QUAI PASTEUR
RUE HAUTE ST-MAURICE
To Bourgueil

9

TOWN MUSEUM
WC
LA MAISON ROUGE
ST. MAURICE
BOOK-SHOP
RUE VOLTAIRE
WALK ENDS
RUE BEAUREPAIRE

10

8

RUE DU GRENIER

12
QUAI CHARLES VII
RUE DU COMMERCE
RUE CARNOT

WOW!

*V i e n n e*

WALK BEGINS
RUE CARNOT

200 Meters
200 Yards

♟ Wine Tasting
← One-Way Street

To Candes-St-Martin by bike

CAMPGROUND

14

QUAI DANTON
To Abbaye Royale de Fontevraud & Château du Rivau

**Accommodations**

1. Best Western Hôtel de France & Au Chapeau Rouge Rest.
2. Hôtel Diderot
3. Le Plantagenêt Hôtel
4. Hôtel la Treille

**Eateries, Wineries & Other**

5. L'Ardoise
6. Un Air d'Antan
7. La Part des Anges
8. La Cave Voltaire

# Sights in Chinon

### Forteresse Royale de Chinon

Chinon's castle (or fortress) is more ruined and older than the more famous and visited châteaux of the Loire. It comes without a hint of pleasure palace. While there's not much left, its rich history and terrific views make the castle a popular destination for historians and French tourists.

LOIRE

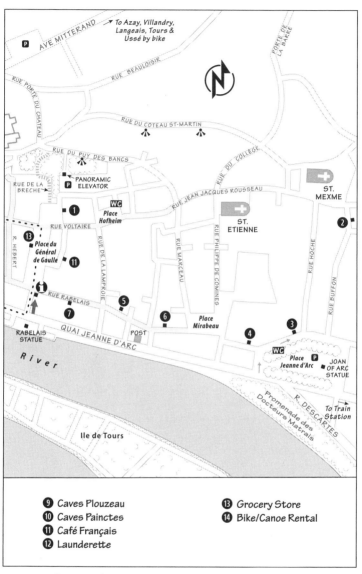

AVE MITTERAND

→ To Azay, Villandry,
Langeais, Tours &
Ussé by bike

PORTE DE
LA BARRE

RUE BEAULOISIR

RUE PORTE DU CHATEAU

RUE DU COTEAU ST-MARTIN

RUE DU PUY DES BANCS

RUE DU COLLEGE

PANORAMIC
ELEVATOR

RUE DE LA
BRECHE →

RUE JEAN JACQUES ROUSSEAU

WC

ST.
MEXME

Place
Hofheim

❶

RUE VOLTAIRE

ST.
ETIENNE

❷

❸

Place du
Général
de Gaulle

RUE DE LA LAMPROIE

RUE MARCEAU

RUE PHILIPPE DE COMINES

RUE HOCHE

RUE BUFFON

R. HEBERT

❶❶

RUE RABELAIS

❺

❼

❻

Place
Mirabeau

POST

❸

QUAI JEANNE D'ARC

❹

RABELAIS
STATUE

WC

Place
Jeanne d'Arc

P

JOAN
OF ARC
STATUE

*River*

R. DESCARTES

Promenade des
Docteurs Matrais

To Train
Station

Ile de Tours

❾ Caves Plouzeau
❿ Caves Painctes
⓫ Café Français
⓬ Launderette

⓭ Grocery Store
⓮ Bike/Canoe Rental

**Cost and Hours:** €10:50, daily 9:30-18:00, May-Aug until 19:00, Nov-Feb until 17:00, +33 2 47 93 13 45, www.forteressechinon.fr.

**Castle Tours:** Your admission includes a HistoPad tablet that leads you through 10 information/entertainment stations. The tablet shows prettified images of how the rooms looked centuries ago (accompanied by fun background noise), but also gives some historical context. Free English-language tours are best to bring the ruins to life. It's worth planning your visit around them (45 minutes, generally at least twice daily March-Oct, check locally for times).

**Getting There:** It's a bracing walk up from town, or walk behind the main square, Place du Général de Gaulle, to find the free "panoramic" elevator (and still climb 5 minutes). A free parking lot is 100 yards above the castle entry.

**Eating:** A garden café with fair prices awaits near the end of your visit.

**Background:** The château has a long and storied history. England's King Henry II and Eleanor of Aquitaine, who ruled a vast realm from Scotland to the Spanish border, reigned from here from 1154 to 1189. They had eight children (among them two future kings, including Richard the Lionheart). The Grand Masters of the Knights Templar were imprisoned here in 1308 before being put to  death in Paris as commanded by the Vatican. (The Knights Templar was a military order of the Catholic Church whose role was to protect Christians in the Holy Land during the early Crusades—but the Church later saw this order as a threat.) And it was here that Joan of Arc pleaded with Charles VII to muster the courage to rally the French and take the throne back from the nasty English. Charles had taken refuge in this well-fortified castle during the Hundred Years' War, making Chinon France's capital city during that low ebb in Gallic history. You'll learn more about these fascinating periods and events during your visit, but you won't see many furnishings.

**Visiting the Castle:** The castle has three structures separated by moats and lots of stone stairs (mostly optional). Enter via the oldest part, the 12th-century Fort Saint-Georges. Crossing a dry moat, you'll land in the big courtyard of the Château du Milieu; at the far end is Fort Coudray. Your first tablet stop is 150 yards to the right when you enter, under the wood shelter.

The fortress comes with commanding views of the town, river, and château-studded countryside. Most of the stones were quarried directly below the castle and hauled up through a well. The resulting caverns keep stores of local wine cool to this day.

Follow *sens de la visite* signs and your tablet through eight stark and stony rooms. There's a small museum devoted to the legendary Joan of Arc and her myth, developed through the centuries to inspire the French to pride and greatness. Chinon—both the city and the castle—developed as its political importance grew. It was the seat of French royalty in the 14th century.

The multifloor dungeon effectively demonstrates how bleak life could be if you landed on the wrong side of the law in the Middle Ages. The last tablet stop is in the slender clock tower, with more steps and more history—but also the grandest views.

## WINE SIGHTS AND TASTINGS

Chinon reds are among the most respected in the Loire. Most of these places are in town and reachable on foot; the last two are outside of town and require a car.

### La Cave Voltaire

At the most convenient of Chinon's wine-tasting options, English-speaking sommelier Florian would love to help you learn about his area's wines. He serves good cheese, *rillettes,* and sausage appetizers and has wines from all regions of France—but the best, of course, are from Chinon. It's a good place to come before dinner or for a light meal. The ambience inside is wine-shop cozy, but the tables outside are hard to resist (Tue-Sun 10:30-23:30, closed Mon, near Place du Général de Gaulle at 13 Rue Voltaire, +33 2 47 93 37 68).

### Caves Plouzeau

This place offers an opportunity to walk through long, atmospheric *caves*—complete with mood lighting—that extend under the château to a (literally) cool tasting room and reasonably priced wines (free tasting, €8-16/bottle; Tue-Sat 11:00-13:00 & 14:00-19:00, Nov-March Tue-Sat 14:00-18:00; closed Sun-Mon year-round; at the western end of town on 94 Rue Haute St-Maurice, +33 2 47 93 16 34, www.plouzeau.com).

### Caves Painctes

At this *cave,* summer travelers can sample Chinon wines and walk through the cool quarry from which stones for the castle and town's houses were cut. This rock (tuff) is soft and easily quarried, and when exposed to oxygen, it hardens. The *caves,* 300 feet directly below the castle, were dug as the castle was built. Its stones were hauled directly up to the building site with a treadmill-powered hoist. Converted to wine cellars in the 15th century, the former quarry is a pilgrimage site of sorts for admirers of Rabelais, who featured it prominently in his writings. The English tour takes about an hour and includes a 20-minute video and a tasting of three local wines. Designed to promote Chinon wines, it's run by a local winemakers' association (€3; July-Aug Tue-Sun at 11:00, 15:00, 16:30, and 18:00; closed Sept-June and Mon year-round; off Rue Voltaire on Impasse des Caves Painctes, +33 2 47 93 30 44).

LOIRE

### Château du Petit Thouars

Château du Petit Thouars offers a fun wine-tasting experience just 10 minutes west of Chinon (near Abbaye Royale de Fontevraud), featuring a castle and vineyards that produce fine white, rosé, and red wines. Drop by for a free tasting or book ahead for a tour and be greeted by the friendly, young, and English-fluent castle owners (French Sébastien and Canadian D'Arcy), who are as excited about this place as you are. Both understand the art of winemaking and love sharing their knowledge (€15 for basic vineyards and cellar tour plus tasting, €10 for more elaborate tasting without tour, €40 for memorable and family-friendly picnic and tasting package, closed Sun; well signed in St-Germain sur Vienne and La Chaussée area—follow the dirt road to the castle; for location see "Near Chinon" map, later; +33 2 47 95 96 40, www.chateaudptwines.com).

### Domaine de la Chevalerie

For an authentic winery experience in the thick of the vineyards, drive about 25 minutes from Chinon to Domaine de la Chevalerie. This traditional winery has been run by the same family for 14 generations. If you're lucky, fun-loving and English-speaking daughter Stéphanie or brother Olivier will take you through the cavernous hillside cellars crammed with 180,000 bottles, then treat you to a tasting of their 100 percent Cabernet Franc reds from seven different plots of land (€15 includes tastes of several wines; visits by appointment only; off D-35 toward Langeais shortly after passing Restigné, look for small red sign on left and then drive a kilometer on a tiny lane, 7 Rue du Peu Muleau, Restigné; for location see the "Near Chinon" map, later, +33 2 47 97 46 32, www.domainedelachevalerie.fr).

## OTHER CHINON ACTIVITIES

### ▲Biking from Chinon

The TI has good fliers on level bike routes from Chinon that combine some bike-only paths with rural lanes and charming villages. The best may be the 12-mile trail (called La Voie Verte) following an abandoned rail line from Chinon to Richelieu. You'll pass near the recommended Château de Rivau as you pedal through fields of sunflowers, small forests, and open pastureland. One downside of this ride is that it's not a loop, like most others, so you return on the same path.

Hardy cyclists can manage the longer ride from Chinon to Ussé and back, and some may want to venture even farther to Villandry. To avoid the monumental hill when leaving town in this direction, take your bike in the free elevator up to the château level, then follow bike icon signs (get directions from your bike shop). Connecting these château towns is a full-day, 40-mile round-trip ride (see the "Near Chinon" map, later, for general route; see "Helpful Hints," earlier, for rental location and costs).

### Canoeing/Kayaking from Chinon
From about April through September, plastic canoes and kayaks are available to rent next to the campground across the lone bridge in Chinon. The outfitters will shuttle you upriver to tiny Anché for a scenic and fun two-hour, four-mile float back to town—ending with great Chinon fortress views. They also offer a 10-mile, half-day float that starts in Chinon and ends downriver in the sweet little village of Candes-St-Martin. Or do your own biathlon by canoeing one way and biking back (see "Helpful Hints," earlier, for rental location and costs).

### Nighttime in Chinon
**Café Français,** run by Jean François (a.k.a. "Jeff"), is a characteristic local hangout and *the* place for late-night fun in this sleepy town (open Tue-Sat from 18:00 and Sun from 19:00 until you shut it down, closed Mon year-round and Sun off-season, live music less likely off-season, behind Town Hall at 37 Rue des Halles, +33 2 47 93 32 78).

## CHATEAUX NEAR CHINON
The best châteaux within day-trip distance of Chinon are Azay-le-Rideau (on an island in a river), Langeais (imposing 15th-century fortress), and Villandry (amazing gardens)—all covered in their own sections later in this chapter. But the following châteaux are also worth consideration.

### Château du Rivau
Gleaming white and medieval, this château sits wedged between wheat and sunflower fields and makes for a memorable 15-minute drive from Chinon—or a lovely 45-minute bike ride (see "Biking from Chinon," earlier). Its owners have spared little expense in their decades-long renovation of the 15th-century castle and its extensive gardens. The 14 different flower and vegetable gardens and orchards are kid-friendly (with elf and fairy guides) and lovingly tended with art installations, topiaries, hammocks, birds, a maze, and more (the medieval castle interior is skippable). A good little café serves reasonable meals in a lovely setting.

**Cost and Hours:** €12, daily 10:00-18:00, May-Sept until 19:00, closed Nov-March, skip the unnecessary audioguide, in Lémeré on D-749—from Chinon follow *Richelieu* signs, then signs to the château; +33 2 47 95 77 47, www.chateaudurivau.com.

### Ussé
This château, famous as an inspiration for Charles Perrault's classic version of the Sleeping Beauty story, is worth a quick photo stop

for its fairy-tale turrets and gardens, but don't bother touring the interior of this pricey pearl. The best view, with reflections and a golden-slipper picnic spot, is just across the bridge and worth a detour to savor.

**Cost and Hours:** €15, daily 10:00-19:00, mid-Feb-March and Sept-mid-Nov until 18:00, closed in winter, along D-7 20 minutes north of Chinon on the Indre River, +33 2 47 95 54 05, www.chateaudusse.fr.

## Sleeping in Chinon

Hotels are a good value in Chinon. If you stay overnight here, walk out to the river and cross the bridge for a floodlit view of the château walls.

**$ Best Western Hôtel de France*** offers good comfort in 28 rooms on Chinon's best square; many have partial views of the fortress (family rooms and suites, several rooms have balconies over the square, some have thin walls, nice courtyard terrace, air-con, easy pay parking near the hotel, 49 Place du Général de Gaulle, +33 2 47 93 33 91, www.bestwestern.fr, hoteldefrance@bw-chinon.fr).

**$ Hôtel Diderot,** a handsome 18th-century manor house on the eastern edge of town, is the closest hotel I list to the train station. This traditional hotel, run by Floridian Jamie and her French husband Jean-Pierre, surrounds a carefully planted courtyard (where you'll park). Rooms in the main building vary in size and decor, but all are well maintained, with personal touches (though no air-conditioning). Ground-floor rooms come with private patios. The  four good family rooms have connecting rooms, each with a private bathroom (limited pay parking, traditional French breakfast, 4 Rue de Buffon, drivers should look for signs from Place Jeanne d'Arc, +33 2 47 93 18 87, www.hoteldiderot.com, hoteldiderot@hoteldiderot.com).

**$ Le Plantagenêt*** has 33 comfortable rooms and may have space when others don't. There's a peaceful if unkept garden courtyard (picnics encouraged if you buy drinks from hotel) and an on-site washer/dryer. Superior rooms in *Maison Bourgeoise* have a more historic feel (air-con, 12 Place Jeanne d'Arc, +33 2 47 93 36 92, www.hotel-plantagenet.com, resa@hotel-plantagenet.com).

**¢ Hôtel la Treille,** run by gregarious Stéphanie, is a true budget place with good-enough rooms at bargain rates. The cheapest share a shower and WC (no air-con, 4 Place Jeanne d'Arc, +33 2 47 93 07 71).

## OUTSIDE CHINON, NEAR LIGRE

**$$ Le Clos de Ligré** lets you sleep in peace, surrounded by vine-yards and farmland. A 10-minute drive from Chinon, it has room to roam, a large pool, and a *salon* library room with a baby grand piano. English-speaking Martine offers cavernous and creatively decorated rooms (good family rooms, includes big breakfast, €40 dinner serves up the works including wine in a traditional setting, 37500 Ligré, +33 2 47 93 95 59, mobile +33 6 61 12 45 55, www.le-clos-de-ligre.com, descamps.ligre@gmail.com). From Chinon, drive toward Richelieu on D-749, turn right on D-115 at the *Ligré par le vignoble* sign, and continue for about five kilometers. Turn left, following signs to *Ligré;* at the Dozon winery turn left and look for signs to *Le Clos de Ligré* (see the "Near Chinon" map, later).

# Eating in Chinon

**$$ Au Chapeau Rouge** offers an elegant yet relaxed *gastronomique* experience for a steal in a lovely dining room or at outdoor tables facing the square. Regional products that change with the season are creatively blended with tradition and beautifully presented (reserve a day ahead or try your luck, closed Sun-Mon, 49 Place du Général de Gaulle, +33 2 47 98 08 08, www.auchapeaurouge.fr).

**$$ L'Ardoise** means "the chalkboard," which is how the menu is presented, reflecting the bistro feel of the place. Dine here to sample carefully prepared, stylishly presented regional cuisine in a lively dining room (closed Mon-Tue, reservations smart, 42 Rue Rabelais, +33 2 47 58 48 78, www.lardoisechinon.com).

**$ Un Air d'Antan** is a tiny, easygoing diner with tasty cuisine at amazing prices, a fun interior, and a small patio (closed Sun-Tue, 54 Bis Rue Rabelais, +33 2 47 95 37 52).

**$$ La Part des Anges** is an intimate two-person love affair with food in a charming setting. Virginie creates contemporary cuisine based on timeless French technique while husband Hervé serves with aplomb (good lunch options, limited outdoor seating, closed Sun-Mon, 5 Rue Rabelais, +33 2 47 93 99 93).

**Groceries: Carrefour City** is across from the Town Hall, on Place du Général de Gaulle (Mon-Sat 7:00-21:00, Sun 9:00-13:00).

## NEAR CHINON

For a memorable countryside meal, drive 25 minutes to **$$ Etape Gourmande** at Domaine de la Giraudière in Villandry (see listing on page 84). A trip here combines well with visits to Villandry and Azay-le-Rideau.

## Chinon Connections

**By Minivan to Loire Châteaux:** Acco-Dispo, Loire Valley Tours, Touraine Evasion, and A La Française Tours offer fixed-itinerary minivan excursions from Tours (see page 36). Take the train to Tours from Chinon (see next), or get several travelers together to book your own van from Chinon.

**By Train/Bus:** Trains and SNCF buses link Chinon daily with **Tours** (8/day, 1 hour, connections to other châteaux and minibus excursions from Tours) and to the regional rail hub of St-Pierre-des-Corps in suburban Tours (TGV trains to distant destinations, and the fastest way to Paris). Traveling by train to the nearby châteaux (except for Azay-le-Rideau) requires careful schedule coordination with a transfer in Tours and healthy walks from the stations to the châteaux. Fewer trains run on weekends.

*To Loire Châteaux:* **Azay-le-Rideau** (7/day, 20 minutes direct, plus long walk to château, or take the slower SNCF bus to the town center near the château, www.sncf-connect.com/bus), **Langeais** (8/day, 2 hours, transfer in Tours), **Amboise** (7/day, 2 hours, transfer in Tours), **Chenonceau** (4/day, 3 hours, transfer in Tours), **Blois** (7/day, 2 hours, transfer in Tours and possibly in St-Pierre-des-Corps).

*To Destinations Beyond the Loire:* **Paris Gare Montparnasse** (8/day, 4 hours, transfer in Tours and sometimes also St-Pierre-des-Corps), **Sarlat-la-Canéda** (3/day, 6-8 hours, change in Tours and St-Pierre-des-Corps, then TGV to Libourne or Bordeaux-St. Jean, then train through Bordeaux vineyards to Sarlat), **Pontorson/Mont St-Michel** (1/day and early, 6 hours with change at Tours main station, Le Mans, and Rennes, then bus from Rennes), **Bayeux** (4/day, 7 hours with change in Tours and Caen, more via Tours, St-Pierre-des-Corps, and Paris leaving from Gare St. Lazare).

# Azay-le-Rideau

This charming 16th-century château, worth ▲▲, sparkles on an island in the Indre River, its image romantically reflected in the slow-moving waters. The building is a prime example of an early-Renaissance château. With no defensive purpose, it was built simply for luxurious living in a luxurious setting. The ornamental facade is perfectly harmonious, and the interior—with its grand staircases and elegant loggias—is Italian-inspired.

Azay-le-Rideau (ah-zay luh ree-doh) is also the name of the

endearing little town, with a small but pleasing pedestrian zone and a fine boutique hotel. It's a good base for bike riders, with its designated bike paths and small roads to nearby châteaux.

**Tourist Information:** Azay-le-Rideau's TI is just below Place de la République, a block to the right of the post office (July-Aug daily 9:30-19:00; April-June and Sept daily 9:30-13:00 & 14:00-18:00; shorter hours Oct-March; 4 Rue du Château, +33 2 47 45 44 40, www.azay-chinon-valdeloire.com). The TI sells reduced-price tickets to all area châteaux and has leads on bike rentals.

## GETTING THERE

Azay-le-Rideau is served by both SNCF trains and buses from Tours (7/day, 30 minutes by train, 1 hour by bus) and Chinon (7/day, 20 minutes by train, 40 minutes by bus). Buses double the travel time but stop in the city center (near the château) and save you the 30-minute walk from the train station (www.sncf-connect.com/bus). From Amboise, it's a doable but long train trip (6/day, 1.5 hours, transfer in Tours).

## ORIENTATION TO CHATEAU D'AZAY-LE-RIDEAU

**Cost and Hours:** €12, daily 9:30-18:00—July-Aug until 19:00, possibly until 23:00 for night visits (see below), Oct-March 10:00-17:15, last entry one hour before closing, storage lockers.

**Information:** +33 2 47 45 42 04, www.azay-le-rideau.fr.

**Tours:** The free and helpful château plan, combined with excellent explanations posted in all rooms, makes the €3 audioguide unnecessary.

**Night Visits** *(Visites Nocturne):* The château may stay open late in summer with fun mood lighting and music to accompany your visit—ask.

**Eating:** The delightful café, just after the château entry, makes a fine lunch or refreshment stop in good weather.

**Flower Garden:** A beautiful flower garden lies opposite the château entry. Look for the sign to *Le Jardin des Secrets*.

## BACKGROUND

The château was built between 1518 and 1527 by a filthy-rich banker—Gilles Berthelot, treasurer to the king of France. The structure

LOIRE

## Near Chinon

**Accommodations**
1 To Le Clos de Ligré
2 Hôtel/Restaurant la Croix Blanche

**Eateries**
3 Etape Gourmande at Domaine de la Giraudière
4 Le Saut aux Loups Mushroom Caves & Rest.

**Wine Tasting**
5 Château du Petit Thouars
6 Domaine de la Chevalerie

has a delightfully feminine touch: Because Gilles was often away for work, his wife, Philippa, supervised the construction. The castle was so lavish that the king, François I, took note, giving it the ultimate compliment: He seized it, causing its owner to flee. Because this château survived the Revolution virtually unscathed, its interior shows three centuries of royal styles. The French government purchased it in 1905.

## VISITING THE CHATEAU

The château plan guides you, starting inside on the first floor up. Rooms are elaborately furnished and decorated but not dissimilar to others you may see in this region. You'll climb to the castle attic *(comble)*, wander under a strikingly beautiful roof support cut from 500-year-old oak trees, and learn about the resident bats hanging around the room (now that's original). Then work your way down through more sumptuous Renaissance rooms loaded with elaborate tapestries, colossal fireplaces, and intricately carved wood chests. Pause to admire the king's portrait gallery in the "Apartement du XVII Siècle" (three Louis, three Henrys, and François I).

For many, the highlight of a visit is the romantic park, designed in the 19th century to enhance the already beautiful châ-

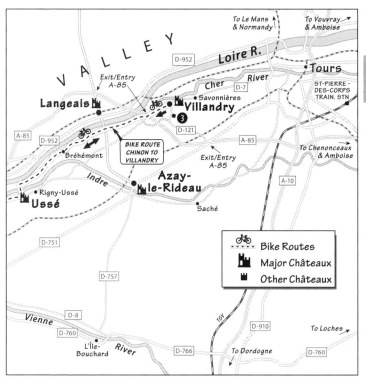

teau. Take a spin on the path around the castle to enjoy romantic views and find the rare-in-France sequoia and cedar trees.

## TOWN OF AZAY-LE-RIDEAU

The town's appealing little center may convince you to set up here. It works well as a base for visiting sights west of Tours by car or bike (but not by train, as the station is a half-mile walk from the town center). It's also close to the A-85 autoroute, offering drivers reasonable access to châteaux near Amboise.

**Sleeping:** Ideally located on a traffic-free street between Place de la République (easy parking) and the château, **$ Hôtel de Biencourt\*\*\*** is a fine choice. This sharp yet affordable boutique hotel has thoughtfully appointed rooms, a pleasing garden terrace, and a calming lounge area (air-con, no elevator, shared fridge, picnics OK on terrace, closed mid-Nov-late March, 7 Rue de Balzac, +33 2 47 45 20 75, www.hoteldebiencourt.fr, contact@hotelbiencourt. fr, helpful owners Xavier and Bruno).

**Eating:** The village has shops with all you need to create a fine picnic. As for restaurants, you'll find fresh and creative cuisine and reasonable prices at **$$ Côté Cour.** Friendly Marius offers a few select choices—local products and mostly organic foods—served in a warm interior or on a great outdoor terrace (good goat-cheese salad, closed Sun, facing the château gate at 19 Rue Balzac, +33 7 71 55 97 27).

**$$ L'Epine** serves some of the finest and best-presented cuisine in town on its generous terrace or in its appealing dining room (book a little ahead for this place, closed Sun-Mon, 19 Place de la République, +33 2 47 45 39 84, www.restaurant-lepine.fr).

**$ L'Epicerie de Julie** is a tiny, inexpensive Italian deli-bistro with a limited but cheap menu and friendly Julie in charge (unpredictable hours but generally until 19:00, usually closed Sun-Mon, 17 Place Gambetta, +33 2 47 42 06 45).

If you have a car, seriously consider the 15-minute drive to dine at **$$$ Domaine de la Giraudière** in Villandry (see "Eating in and near Villandry," later).

# Langeais

One of the most imposing-looking fortresses of the Middle Ages, Château de Langeais—rated ▲—was built mostly for show. Dominating its appealing little village, it comes with a moat, a drawbridge, lavish defenses, and turrets.

## GETTING THERE

Trains link Langeais with Tours (7/day, 15 minutes). Connections from Chinon and Azay-le-Rideau are challenging. Consider renting an e-bike, as it's a lovely ride on mostly quiet lanes and bike paths.

The A-85 autoroute provides convenient access for drivers coming from points east or west. Drivers should turn right at the foot of the castle, then hug the castle; the parking area is 200 yards past the château, on the right.

## ORIENTATION TO CHATEAU DE LANGEAIS

**Cost and Hours:** €11, daily July-Aug 9:00-19:00, April-June and Sept-mid-Nov 9:30-18:30, mid-Nov-March 10:00-17:00, last entry one hour before closing, +33 2 47 96 72 60, www. chateau-de-langeais.com.

**Eating:** The château is within easy walking distance of several cafés and restaurants.

**Services:** WCs are in the courtyard, opposite the entry.

## BACKGROUND

Langeais occupies a key site on the Loire River, 15 miles downstream on the road to Tours (which for a time was the French capital), and about halfway from Paris along the trading route to Brittany and the Atlantic. This location made Langeais a player

in historic events, though the only remaining part of the original castle is the thousand-year-old tower standing across from the castle's garden. (That castle, an English stronghold, was destroyed by the French king in the Hundred Years' War.)

The "new" castle, built in the 15th century, dates from the age of cannons, which would have made quick work of its tough-looking facade. In fact, the imposing walls were mostly for show. This is a transitional piece of architecture: part medieval and part Renaissance. The mullioned windows overlooking the courtyard indicate this was a fancy residence more than a defensive fortress. While Langeais makes a show of its defenses, castles built just 50 years later (such as Azay-le-Rideau) give not a hint of fortification.

## VISITING THE CHATEAU

The interior is late Middle Ages chic. It's the life's work of a 19th-century owner who was a lover of medieval art. He decorated and furnished the rooms with 15th- and 16th-century artifacts or good facsimiles. Most of what you see is modern-made in 16th-century style.

Langeais tries hard to give visitors a feel for royal life in the 15th century—and it succeeds. The palace is decked out as palaces were—designed to impress, and ready to pack and move. The rooms are well furnished and well explained with handy information sheets (or with a good booklet you may need to ask for, if the sheets aren't out). The video in the first room sets the stage for your visit.

As you tour the castle, pay attention to the exquisite floor tiles and colorful, beamed ceilings. The first rooms are filled with fine tapestries, foldable chairs, and big chests with handles, all of which could have been set up in a matter of hours. Big-time landowners circulated through their domains, moving every month or so. Also notice how each piece of furniture had multiple uses—such as a throne that doubled as a writing desk or storage space.

The **banquet room** table would have groaned with food and luxury items—but just one long, communal napkin and no forks (in the 16th century Catherine de' Medici brought her table manners—including using forks and individual napkins—to France). Belgian tapestries on the walls still glimmer with 500-year-old silk thread. In an upstairs **bedroom,** it looks like the master has just left—gloves and other accessories are lying on the bedcovers, and shoes sit below the bed. There were bedrooms for show, and bedrooms for sleeping.

In the **Wedding Hall,** wax figures re-create the historic marriage that gave Langeais its 15 minutes of château fame in 1491. It was here that 21-year-old King Charles VIII secretly wed 14-year-old Anne (duchess of Brittany), a union that brought independent Brittany into France's fold. The gowns are accurate and impressive, and it's amusing to see how short everyone was in the Middle Ages—which explains the short beds. A projection narrated by the castle owner explains the event (no subtitles—yet).

The dark top-floor museum has a rare series of 16th-century **tapestries** featuring nine heroes—biblical, Roman, and medieval. This is one of just three such sets in existence, with seven of the original nine scenes surviving. Leave this room by the doors in the center of the room on the left and complete your visit with commanding **town views** from the impressive ramparts, then descend, passing more rooms (including one that sells small tapestry samples). Once outside, you'll find that the hillside gardens give terrific views back to the castle. Stairs behind the ruined wall lead up to the best views.

# Villandry

Château de Villandry (vee-lahn-dree) is famous for its extensive gardens, considered to be the best in the Loire Valley and possibly all of France. Its château is me-
diocre by Loire Valley standards, but
the grounds—arranged in elaborate
geometric patterns and immaculately
maintained—make it a ▲▲ sight
(worth ▲▲▲ for gardeners). Still, if
you're visiting anyway, it's worth the
extra euros to tour the château as well.

## GETTING THERE
There is no train station here. In summer, buses run twice a day from the
train station in Tours to Villandry,
though the best no-car option is to
take a minivan excursion from Amboise or Tours (see page 36). The
scenic bike trail that passes by Villandry makes it a popular destination for cyclists (2 hours from Chinon, 1 hour from Azay-le-Rideau).

Drivers will find free parking located across from the entry (hide valuables in your trunk). Villandry's **TI** (with a few bikes to rent) is in the village, a few hundred yards west of the château (1 Rue Principale, +33 2 47 50 12 66).

## ORIENTATION TO CHATEAU DE VILLANDRY

**Cost and Hours:** €12, €7.50 for gardens only; daily 9:00-18:00, Nov-mid-Feb 10:00-17:00.

**Information:** +33 2 47 50 02 09, www.chateauvillandry.fr.

**Tours:** The excellent handout leads you through the château's 19th-century rooms. Skip the unnecessary €4 audioguide.

**Services:** Storage lockers are available.

**Gardens:** You can stay as late as you like in the gardens, though you must enter before the ticket office closes and exit through the back gate after 19:00.

**Eating:** You'll find a good café at the entry and more choices 200 yards down the road in the village.

## BACKGROUND

Finished in 1536, Villandry was the last great Renaissance château built on the Loire. It's yet another pet project of a fabulously wealthy finance minister of François I—Jean le Breton. While serving as ambassador to Italy, Jean fell in love with Italian Renaissance gardens. When he took over this property, he razed the 12th-century castle (keeping only the old tower), put up his own château, and installed a huge Italian-style garden. The château was purchased in 1906 by the present owner's great-grandfather, and the garden—a careful reconstruction of what the original might have been—is the result of three generations of passionate dedication.

## VISITING THE CHATEAU AND GARDENS

The **château**'s 19th-century rooms feel so lived-in that you'll wonder if the family just stepped out to get their poodle bathed. Don't miss the 15-minute *Four Seasons of Villandry* slideshow just inside the château. With period music and narration by the château owner, it delivers a glimpse at the gardens throughout the year in a relaxing little theater (ask at the ticket window or you may miss it—and ask for the version with subtitles). The literal high point of your château visit is the spiral climb to the top of the keep—the only surviving part of the medieval castle—where you'll find a 360-degree view of the gardens, village, and surrounding countryside. The extra cost for visiting the château seems worth it when you take in the panorama.

The lovingly tended **gardens** are well described by your handout. Follow its recommended route through the four garden types. The 10-acre Renaissance garden, inspired by the 1530s Italian-style original, is full of symbolism. Even the herb and vegetable sections are arranged with artistic flair. The earliest Loire gardens were practical, grown by medieval abbey monks who needed vegetables to feed their community and medicinal herbs to cure their ailments. And those monks liked geometrical patterns. Later Italian influence brought decorative ponds, tunnels, and fountains. Harmonizing the flowers and vegetables was an innovation of 16th-century Loire châteaux. This example is the closest we have to that garden style. Who knew that lentils, chives, and cabbages could look this good?

The 85,000 plants—half of which come from the family greenhouse—are replanted twice a year by 10 full-time gardeners. They use modern organic methods: ladybugs instead of pesticides and a whole lot of hoeing. The place is as manicured as a putting green—just try to find a weed. Stroll under the grapevine trellis, through a good-looking salad zone, and among Anjou pears (from the nearby region of Angers). If all the topiary and straight angles seem too rigid, look for the sun garden in the back of the estate, which has "wilder" perennial borders favored by the Brits. Charts posted throughout identify everything in English.

Bring bread for the piranha-like carp who prowl the fanciful moat. Like the carp swimming around other Loire châteaux, they're so voracious, they'll gather at your feet to frantically eat your spit. Don't miss the fine views from the Belvedere lookout (near the garden exit).

## EATING IN AND NEAR VILLANDRY

The pleasant little village of Villandry has several cafés and restaurants, a small grocery store, and a bakery.

**$$ Etape Gourmande at Domaine de la Giraudière** offers a wonderfully rustic farmhouse dining experience. Gentle owner Alexandra takes time with every client, and the country-gourmet cuisine is simply delicious. The dining room is hunting-lodge cozy, and there's nice outdoor seating under the shade of generous trees (12:00-14:30 & 19:30-21:00, closed Wed and mid-Nov-mid-March, reservations smart, a half-mile from Villandry's château toward Druye; for location see the "Near Chinon" map, earlier; +33 2 47 50 08 60, www.letapegourmande.com). This place works well for lunch, as it's well signed between Villandry and Azay-le-Rideau on D-121.

# Abbaye Royale de Fontevraud

The Royal Abbey of Fontevraud (fohn-tuh-vroh), worth ▲, is a 15-minute journey west from Chinon. This once-vast 12th-century abbey provides keen insight into medieval monastic life. The "abbey" was actually a 12th-century monastic city, the largest such compound in Europe—with four monastic complexes, all within a fortified wall. A dazzling new museum of modern art on-site is well worth your time.

## ORIENTATION

**Cost and Hours:** €12 for abbey, €6 for museum, €15 for both; daily 9:30-19:00, Nov-March until 18:00, closed Jan.

**Information:** +33 2 41 51 73 52, www.fontevraud.fr.

**Tours:** English information panels are posted throughout the abbey and art museum, making the well-done €4.50 audioguide inessential. Kids love the iPad "treasure hunt" (€4.50).

**Parking:** Park free at the first "P" lot you see as you approach the abbey—in the large, tree-lined square.

## BACKGROUND

The order of Fontevraud, founded in 1101, was an experiment of rare audacity. This was a double monastery, where both men and women lived under the authority of an abbess while observing the rules of St. Benedict (but influenced by the cult of the Virgin Mary). Men and women lived separately and chastely within the abbey walls. The order thrived, and in the 16th century, this was the administrative head of more than 150 monasteries. Four communities lived within these walls until the Revolution. In 1804, Napoleon made the abbey a prison, which ironically helped preserve the building. It functioned as a prison for 150 years, until 1963, with five wooden floors filled with cells. Designed to house 800 inmates, the prison was notoriously harsh.

## VISITING THE ABBEY

Follow *sens de la visite* signs to tour the abbey (basically clockwise).

Your visit begins in the bright, 12th-century, Romanesque **abbey church.** Sit inside on the steps, savor the ethereal setting, and feel the power of this Romanesque structure. Appreciate the finely carved capitals and read the big-screen monitors. At the end of the nave are four painted sarcophagi belonging to Eleanor of Aquitaine; her second husband, Henry II, the first of England's Plantagenet kings; their son

Richard the Lionheart; and his sister-in-law. These are the tops of the sarcophagi only. Even though we know these Plantagenets were buried here (they were big donors to the abbey), no one knows the fate of the actual bodies.

Pause again by the altar to admire the rounded arches and the scale of the church, then leave through the right transept into the spacious **cloister.** This was the center of the abbey, where the nuns read, exercised, checked their Twitter feeds, and washed their hands. While visiting the abbey, remember that monastic life was darn simple: nothing but prayers, readings, and work. Daily rations were a loaf of bread and a half-liter of wine per person, plus soup and smoked fish. English information panels in this section describe the many abbesses who ran the show for centuries.

The **chapter house,** on the left as you enter the cloister, is where the nuns' meetings took place. Renaissance paintings feature the Passion of Christ and highlight the women who ran this abbey. The **community room/treasury** comes next. It's the only heated room in the abbey, where the nuns embroidered linen and where today you'll see gripping fragments from a 12th-century Last Judgment and other important abbey treasures—as well as excellent information on the history of the abbey.

Climb steps up to see the cavernous **Grand Dortoir** (dormitory), where hundreds of monks could sleep under a massive wood-beamed ceiling. You'll likely find rotating exhibits here and in an adjacent room. Climb more steps and open the door to peer into the auditorium, with another impressive ceiling. Back down the steps, the **refectory,** built to feed 400 silent monks at a time, was later the prison work yard, where inmates built wooden chairs (exposition rooms above provide insight into this period).

Your abbey visit continues with the unusual, honeycombed, 12th-century **kitchen** (accessed from outside), with five bays covered by 18 chimneys to evacuate smoke. It likely served as a smokehouse for fish farmed in the abbey ponds. Abbeys like this were industrious places, but focused on self-sufficiency rather than trade.

Finish your visit with a refreshment at the **garden café** or in the fancy hotel below, and contemplate a wander through the abbey's **medicinal gardens.**

**Fontevraud Modern Art Museum:** Opened in 2021, this is hands-down the most enjoyable modern-art museum I have visited. The well-curated, beautifully displayed art comes from a private collection donated to the Loire region. You'll see selected works from well-known artists like Toulouse-Lautrec, Degas, Rodin, Derain, and Dufy. More important, though, this place turned me on to artists whose names I had never heard. Paintings, primitive art, blown glass, and sculpture are creatively juxtaposed in an effort to stimulate and provoke your perception. Read the excellent flier that describes the collection and the periods and styles it covers.

## SLEEPING AND EATING

**$$ Hôtel la Croix Blanche,**\*\*\* run by affable and English-fluent Mieke and Christoph, welcomes travelers with flowery terraces and cushy comfort. This fun restaurant-hotel, just outside the abbey, combines a stylish hunting-lodge feel with comfortable public spaces, a pool, and 24 rooms of various sizes, some ideal for families (Place Plantagenêts—see the "Near Chinon" map, earlier; +33 2 41 51 71 11, www.hotel-croixblanche.com, bonjour@hotel-croixblanche.com).

The abbey faces the main square of a charming little town with several handy eateries, a grocery shop, and a wine bar. The *boulangerie* opposite the entrance to the abbey serves tasty quiche and sandwiches at good prices, but you'll find other options as well.

**$$ Restaurant la Croix Blanche** owns a pleasing, casual interior and a reputation for very well-prepared cuisine at fair prices (daily, 5 Place des Plantagenets, +33 2 41 51 71 11).

## NEAR FONTEVRAUD: MUSHROOM CAVES

For an unusual fungus find close to the abbey of Fontevraud, visit the mushroom caves called **Le Saut aux Loups.** France is one of the world's top mushroom producers, so mushrooms matter. Climb to a cliff ledge and stroll through 16 chilly rooms bored into limestone to discover everything about the care and nurturing of mushrooms. You'll see them raised in planters, plastic bags, logs, and straw bales, and you'll learn about their incubation, pasteurization, and fermentation. Abandoned limestone quarries like this are fertile homes for mushroom cultivation and have made the Loire Valley the mushroom capital of France since the 1800s. Ogle the weird shapes—you'll never take your 'shrooms for granted again. The growers harvest a ton of mushrooms each month in these caves; shiitakes are their most important crop. Pick up the English booklet and follow the fungus. Many visitors come only for the on-site mushroom restaurant, whose wood-fired *galipettes* (stuffed mushrooms with crème fraîche and herbs) are the kitchen's forte (€12 for three *galipettes*).

**Cost and Hours:** €7.50, daily 10:00-18:00, July-Aug until 19:00, closed mid-Nov-Feb, dress warmly, just north of Fontevraud at Montsoreau's west end along the river, for location see the "Near Chinon" map, earlier, +33 2 41 51 70 30, www.troglo-sautauxloups.com.

# PRACTICALITIES

This section covers just the basics on traveling in France (for more comprehensive information, see the latest edition of *Rick Steves France*). You'll find free advice on specific topics at RickSteves. com/tips.

## LANGUAGE

Many French people—especially in the tourism industry—speak English, but if you use just a few French phrases, you'll get more smiles and make more friends. In France, it's essential to acknowledge the person before getting down to business. Start any conversation, or enter any shop, by saying: *"Bonjour, madame (*or *monsieur)."* To ask if they speak English, say, *"Parlez-vous anglais?"* For more helpful words to know, see "Survival Phrases" at the end of this chapter.

## MONEY

France uses the euro currency: 1 euro (€) = about $1.10. To convert prices in euros to dollars, add about 10 percent: €20 = about $22, €50 = about $55. (Check www.oanda.com for the latest exchange rates.)

You'll use your **credit card** for purchases both big (hotels, advance tickets) and small (little shops, food stands). Visa and Mastercard are universal while American Express and Discover are less common. Some European businesses have gone cashless, making a card your only payment option.

A **"tap-to-pay"** or "contactless" card is the most widely accepted and simplest to use: Before departing, check if you have—or can get—a tap-to-pay credit card (look on the card for the symbol—four curvy lines) and consider setting up your smartphone for contactless payment. Let your bank know that you'll be traveling in Europe, adjust your ATM withdrawal limit if needed, and make sure you know the four-digit PIN for each of your cards, both debit and credit (as you may need to use **chip-and-PIN** for certain purchases). Allow time to receive your PIN by mail.

While most transactions are by card these days, **cash** can help you out of a jam if your card randomly doesn't work, and can be useful to pay for tips and local guides. Wait until you arrive to get euros using your **debit card** (airports have plenty of cash machines). European ATMs accept US debit cards with a Visa or Mastercard logo and work just like they do at home—except they spit out local currency instead of dollars. When possible, withdraw cash from a bank-run ATM located just outside that bank (they usually charge lower fees and are more secure).

Whether withdrawing cash at an ATM or paying with a credit card, you'll often be asked whether you want the transaction processed in dollars or in the local currency. To avoid a poor exchange rate, always refuse the conversion and *choose the local currency*.

Although rare, some US cards may not work at self-service payment machines (such as transit-ticket kiosks, tollbooths, or fuel pumps). Usually a tap-to-pay card does the trick in these situations. Carry cash as a backup and look for a cashier who can process your payment if your card is rejected.

Before you leave home, let your bank know when and where you'll be using your credit and debit cards. To keep your cash, cards, and valuables safe when traveling, wear a **money belt**.

## STAYING CONNECTED

The simplest solution is to bring your own device—mobile phone, tablet, or laptop—and use it just as you would at home (following the money-saving tips below). For more on phoning, see RickSteves.com/phoning. For a one-hour talk covering tech issues for travelers, see RickSteves.com/mobile-travel-skills.

**To Call from a US Phone:** Phone numbers in this book are presented exactly as you would dial them from a US mobile phone. For international access, press and hold the 0 key until you get a + sign, then dial the country code (33 for France) and phone number (omit the initial zero that's used for domestic calls). To dial from a US landline, replace + with 011 (US/Canada international access code).

**From a European Landline:** Replace + with 00 (Europe international access code), then dial the country code (33 for France) and phone number (omitting the initial zero).

**Within France:** To place a domestic call (from a French land-

## Sleep Code

Hotels are classified based on the average price of a standard double room without breakfast in high season.

| | |
|---|---|
| $$$$ | **Splurge:** Most rooms over €300 |
| $$$ | **Pricier:** €200-300 |
| $$ | **Moderate:** €130-200 |
| $ | **Budget:** €70-130 |
| ¢ | **Backpacker:** Under €70 |
| RS% | **Rick Steves discount** |
| * | **French hotel rating system** (0-5 stars) |

Unless otherwise noted, credit cards are accepted, hotel staff speak basic English, and free Wi-Fi is available. Comparison-shop by checking prices at several hotels (on each hotel's own website, on a booking site, or by email). For the best deal, *book directly with the hotel.* Ask for a discount if paying in cash; if the listing includes **RS%,** request a Rick Steves discount.

line or mobile), drop the +33 and dial the phone number (including the initial zero).

**Tips:** If you bring your mobile phone, consider signing up for an international plan; most providers offer a simple bundle that includes calling, messaging, and data.

Use Wi-Fi (pronounced *wee-fee* in French) whenever possible. Most hotels and many cafés offer free Wi-Fi, and you may also find it at tourist information offices (TIs), major museums, public-transit hubs, aboard trains and buses, and at some autoroute (highway) rest stops. With Wi-Fi you can use your device to make free or low-cost calls via a calling app such as Skype, WhatsApp, FaceTime, and Google Meet. When you need to get online but can't find Wi-Fi, turn on your cellular network (or turn off airplane mode) just long enough for the task at hand.

Most **hotels** charge a fee for placing calls—ask for rates before you dial. Prepaid international phone cards *(cartes international)* are not widely used in France, but can be found at some newsstands, tobacco shops, and train stations.

## SLEEPING

I've categorized my recommended accommodations based on price, indicated with a dollar-sign rating (see sidebar). Book your accommodations as soon as your itinerary is set, especially if you want to stay at one of my top listings or if you'll be traveling during busy times. You can do this by checking hotel websites and booking sites such as Hotels.com or Booking.com. In France, May and September bring larger crowds.

Once your dates are set, compare prices at several hotels. You can do this by checking hotel websites and booking sites such as

Hotels.com or Booking.com. After you've zeroed in on your choice, **book directly with the hotel itself.** This increases the chances that the hotelier will be able to accommodate special needs or requests (such as shifting your reservation). And when you book on the hotel's website, by email, or by phone, the owner avoids the commission paid to booking sites, giving them wiggle room to offer you a discount, a nicer room, or a free breakfast.

For family-run hotels, it's generally best to book your room directly via email or phone. Here's what they'll want to know: number and type of rooms; number of nights; arrival date; departure date; any special requests; and applicable discounts (such as a Rick Steves discount, cash discount, or promotional rate). Use the European style for writing dates: day/month/year.

The French have a simple hotel-rating system based on amenities (one through five stars, one being modest, and indicated in this book by * through *****). Two- and three-star hotels are my mainstays and offer most of the comforts. Other accommodation options include bed-and-breakfasts (*chambres d'hôtes,* usually cheaper than hotels), hostels, campgrounds, or vacation homes (*gîtes,* rented by the week). For a list of over 21,000 *chambres d'hôtes* throughout France, check www.chambres-hotes.fr. To find an apartment or room in a private home, try Airbnb, FlipKey, Booking.com, VRBO, InterhomeUSA.com, and RentaVilla.com.

Room prices can fluctuate significantly with demand and amenities (size, views, room class, and so on), but relative price categories remain constant. Hotels in France must charge a daily tax *(taxe du séjour)* of about €1-4 per person per day (based on the number of stars the hotel has).

Some hotels extend a discount to those who pay cash or stay longer than three nights. And some accommodations offer a special discount for Rick Steves readers, indicated in this guidebook by the abbreviation "**RS%**."

## EATING

I've categorized my recommended eateries based on the average price of a typical main course, indicated with a dollar-sign rating (see sidebar). The cuisine is a highlight of any French adventure. It's sightseeing for your palate. For a formal meal, go to a restaurant or bistro. If you want the option of lighter fare (just soup or a sandwich), head for a café or brasserie instead.

French restaurants usually open for dinner at 19:00 and are most crowded about 20:00 (21:00 in cities). Last seating is usually about 21:00 or 22:00. If a restaurant serves lunch, it generally begins at 12:00 and goes until 14:00, with last orders taken at about 13:30.

In France, an *entrée* is the first course, a *plat principal* is the

**PRACTICALITIES**

---

## Restaurant Code

Eateries in this book are categorized according to the average cost of a typical main course. Drinks, desserts, and splurge items can raise the price considerably.

| | |
|---|---|
| $$$$ | **Splurge:** Most main courses over €40 |
| $$$ | **Pricier:** €30-40 |
| $$ | **Moderate:** €20-30 |
| $ | **Budget:** Under €20 |

In France, a crêpe stand or other takeout spot is **$;** a sit-down brasserie, café, or bistro with affordable *plats du jour* is **$$;** a casual but more upscale restaurant is **$$$;** and a swanky splurge is **$$$$.**

---

main course. *Plats* are generally more meat-based, while *entrées* usually include veggies. It's common to order only a *plat principal*—and maybe a dessert. If you ask for the *menu* (muh-noo), you won't get a list of dishes; you'll get a fixed-price meal—usually two, three, or four courses. With a three-course *menu* you'll choose a starter of soup, appetizer, or salad; select from three or four main courses with vegetables; and finish up with a cheese course and/or a choice of desserts. Drinks are extra. If you want to see a menu and order à la carte, ask for *la carte* (lah kart). Request the waiter's help in deciphering the French.

French cafés and brasseries provide user-friendly meals, but they're not necessarily cheaper than many restaurants and bistros. Famous cafés on popular squares can be pricey affairs. If you're hungry between lunch and dinner (when restaurants are closed) go to a brasserie, which generally serves throughout the day (usually with a limited menu during off-hours). Some cafés serve all day, but those in small towns often close their kitchens from 14:00 to 18:00. The key advantage of cafés and brasseries is flexibility: They offer long serving hours, and you're welcome to order just a salad, a sandwich, or a bowl of soup, even for dinner. Check the price list first, which by law should be posted. There are two sets of prices: You'll pay more for the same drink if you're seated at a table *(salle)* than if you're seated or standing at the bar or counter *(comptoir).*

**Tipping:** At cafés and restaurants, a 12-15 percent service charge is always included in the price of what you order *(service compris* or *prix net),* but you won't see it listed on your bill. If you feel the service was good, tip a little—about 5 percent (maybe 10 percent for terrific service). France pays servers a decent wage and most locals only tip a little, or not at all—so never feel guilty if you don't leave a tip. Tip in cash—credit-card receipts don't have a space for adding tips.

**Breakfast:** Most hotels serve an optional breakfast (generally €10-20). They almost all offer a buffet (cereal, yogurt, fruit, cheese, ham, croissants, juice, and hard-boiled eggs). Coffee is often self-serve from a machine or a thermos. If all you want is coffee or tea and a croissant, the corner café or bakery offers more atmosphere and is less expensive (though you get more coffee at your hotel).

## TRANSPORTATION

**By Train:** Travelers who need to cover long distances in France by train can get a good deal with a Eurail France Pass, sold only outside Europe. To see if a rail pass could save you money, check RickSteves.com/rail. For train schedules, visit Germany's all-Europe website (www.bahn.com) or France's SNCF (www.sncf.com); for online ticket sales, go to https://en.oui.sncf/en or use the SNCF app, which is a great tool for looking up schedules and buying tickets (you'll receive a QR code for your trip, which the conductor will scan onboard). You can also buy tickets at train-station ticket windows or from ticket machines (at most stations). While most machines accept American credit cards if you know your PIN, be prepared with euro coins and bills just in case.

All **high-speed TGV trains** in France (also called "InOui") require a seat reservation—book as early as possible, as these trains fill fast. Tickets go on sale four months in advance, with a wide range of prices. The cheapest tickets sell out early and reservations for rail-pass holders also get more expensive as seats fill up.

At major stations you'll need to scan your ticket at turnstiles to access the tracks. Smaller stations continue to use the old system of validating your ticket in yellow machines near the platform or waiting area. Print-at-home tickets and etickets don't require validation—just show your QR code to the conductor on the train.

Strikes *(grève)* in France are common but generally last no longer than a day or two; ask your hotelier if one is coming.

**By Bus:** Regional buses work well for many destinations not served by trains. Buses are almost always comfortable and air-conditioned. For cheap long-distance bus fares between cities in France, check out www.flixbus.com and www.blablacar.fr.

**By Plane:** Covering long distances on a budget flight can be cheaper than a train or bus ride (though it leaves a larger carbon footprint). Check the cost of a flight on one of Europe's airlines, whether a major carrier or a no-frills outfit like EasyJet or Ryanair. Kayak is the top site for flights to and within Europe, easy-to-use Google Flights has price alerts, and Skyscanner includes many inexpensive flights within Europe.

**By Car:** It's cheaper to arrange most car rentals from the US. For tips on your insurance options, see RickSteves.com/cdw. Bring your driver's license.

Local road etiquette is similar to that in the US. Ask your car-rental company for details, or check the US State Department website (www.travel.state.gov, search for France in the "Learn about your destination" box, then select "Travel and Transportation").

It's also required that you carry an International Driving Permit (IDP), available at your local AAA office ($20 plus two passport-type photos, www.aaa.com).

France's toll road *(autoroute)* system is slick and speedy, but pricey; two hours of driving costs about €15 in tolls. Pay cash (coins or bills under €50) at toll booths, since some US credit cards won't work. Follow the coins icon (usually in white; coins and cards accepted) to enter the toll booth. If you don't see these icons, take the green-arrow lane.

A car is a worthless headache in cities—park it safely (get tips from your hotelier). As break-ins are common, be sure your valuables are out of sight and locked in the trunk, or even better, with you or in your hotel room.

## HELPFUL HINTS

**Travel Advisories:** Before traveling, check updated health and safety conditions, including restrictions for your destination, on the travel pages of the US State Department (www.travel.state.gov) and Centers for Disease Control and Prevention (www.cdc.gov/travel). The US embassy websites for France are also good sources of information (see below).

**Covid Vaccine/Test Requirements:** It's possible you'll need to present proof of vaccination against the coronavirus and/or a negative Covid-19 test result to board a plane to Europe or back to the US. Carefully check requirements for each country you'll visit well before you depart, and again a few days before your trip. See the websites listed above for current requirements.

**Emergency and Medical Help:** For any emergency service—ambulance, police, or fire—call **112** from a mobile phone or landline (operators typically speak English). For hearing-assisted help for all services, dial 114. If you get sick, do as the French do and go to a pharmacist for advice. Or ask at your hotel for help—they'll know the nearest medical and emergency services.

For **passport problems,** contact the **US Embassy** (Paris—appointment required, dial +33 1 43 12 22 22, https://fr.usembassy.gov; Marseille—appointment required, dial +33 1 43 12 47 54, https://fr.usembassy.gov/embassy-consulates/marseille) or the **Canadian Embassy** (Paris—appointment required, dial +33 1 44 43 29 00, Nice—dial +33 4 93 13 17 19; www.canadainternational.gc.ca/france).

**ETIAS Registration:** The European Union may soon require US and Canadian citizens to register online with the European Travel Information and Authorization System (ETIAS) before entering Spain, France, and other Schengen Zone countries (quick and easy process). For the latest, check www.etiasvisa.com.

**Theft or Loss:** France has hardworking pickpockets, and they particularly target those coming in from Paris airports—wear a money belt. Assume beggars are pickpockets and any scuffle is simply a distraction by a team of thieves. If you stop for any commotion or show, put your hands in your pockets before someone else does.

To replace a passport, you'll need to go in person to an embassy or consulate (see above). Cancel and replace your credit and debit cards by calling these 24-hour US numbers with a mobile phone: Visa (dial +1 303 967 1096), MasterCard (dial +1 636 722 7111), and American Express (dial +1 336 393 1111). From a landline, you can call these US numbers collect by going through a local operator.

File a police report either on the spot or within a day or two; you'll need it to submit an insurance claim for lost or stolen items, and it can help with replacing your passport or credit and debit cards. For more information, see RickSteves.com/help.

**Time:** France uses the 24-hour clock. It's the same through 12:00 noon, then keep going: 13:00, 14:00, and so on. France, like most of continental Europe, is six/nine hours ahead of the East/West Coasts of the US.

**Business Hours:** Much of rural France is closed weekdays from 12:00 to 14:00 (lunch is sacred). On Sunday, most businesses are closed (family is sacred), though some small shops such as *boulangeries* (bakeries) are open until noon, special events and weekly markets pop up, and museums are open all day (but public transit options are limited). On Mondays, some businesses are closed until 14:00 and possibly all day. Touristy shops are usually open daily.

**Sightseeing:** Many popular sights come with long lines—not to get in, but to buy a ticket. Visitors who buy tickets online in advance (or who have a museum pass covering these key sights) can skip the line and waltz right in. Advance tickets are generally timed-entry, meaning you're guaranteed admission on a certain date and time.

For some sights, buying ahead is required (tickets aren't sold at the sight and it's the only way to get in). At other sights, buying ahead is recommended to skip the line and save time. And for many sights, advance tickets are available but unnecessary: At these uncrowded sights you can simply arrive, buy a ticket, and go in.

Use my advice in this book as a guide. Note any must-see sights that sell out long in advance and be prepared to buy tickets early. If you do your research, you'll know the smart strategy.

Given how precious your vacation time is, I'd book in advance both where it's required (as soon as your dates are firm) and where it will save time in a long line (in some cases, you can do this even on the day you plan to visit).

**Holidays and Festivals:** France celebrates many holidays, which can close sights and attract crowds (book hotel rooms ahead). For information on holidays and festivals, check France's website: http://us.france.fr. For a simple list showing major—though not all—events, see RickSteves.com/festivals.

**Numbers and Stumblers:** What Americans call the second floor of a building is the first floor in Europe. Europeans write dates as day/month/year, so Christmas 2023 is 25/12/23. Commas are decimal points and vice versa—a dollar and a half is 1,50, a thousand is 1.000, and there are 5.280 feet in a mile. France uses the metric system: A kilogram is 2.2 pounds; a liter is about a quart; and a kilometer is six-tenths of a mile.

## RESOURCES FROM RICK STEVES

This Snapshot guide, excerpted from my latest edition of *Rick Steves France,* is one of many titles in my series of guidebooks on European travel. I also produce a public television series, *Rick Steves' Europe,* and a public radio show, *Travel with Rick Steves.* My free online video library, Rick Steves Classroom Europe, offers a searchable database of short video clips on European history, culture, and geography (Classroom.RickSteves.com). My website, RickSteves.com, offers free travel information, a forum for travelers' comments, guidebook updates, my travel blog, an online travel store, and information on European rail passes and our tours of Europe. If you're bringing a mobile device, you can download my free Rick Steves Audio Europe app that features dozens of self-guided audio tours of the top sights in Europe and travel interviews about France. For more information, see RickSteves.com/audioeurope. You can also follow me on Facebook, Twitter, and Instagram.

## ADDITIONAL RESOURCES

**Tourist Information:** http://us.france.fr
**Passports and Red Tape:** www.travel.state.gov
**Packing List:** www.ricksteves.com/packing
**Travel Insurance:** www.ricksteves.com/insurance
**Cheap Flights:** www.kayak.com or www.google.com/flights
**Airplane Carry-on Restrictions:** www.tsa.gov
**Updates for This Book:** www.ricksteves.com/update

## HOW WAS YOUR TRIP?

To share your tips, concerns, and discoveries after using this book, please fill out the survey at RickSteves.com/feedback. Thanks in advance—it helps a lot.

# French Survival Phrases

When using the phonetics, try to nasalize the n sound.

| | | |
|---|---|---|
| **Good day.** | Bonjour. | bohn-zhoor |
| **Mrs. / Mr.** | Madame / Monsieur | mah-dahm / muhs-yuh |
| **Do you speak English?** | Parlez-vous anglais? | par-lay-voo ahn-glay |
| **Yes. / No.** | Oui. / Non. | wee / nohn |
| **I understand.** | Je comprends. | zhuh kohn-prahn |
| **I don't understand.** | Je ne comprends pas. | zhuh nuh kohn-prahn pah |
| **Please.** | S'il vous plaît. | see voo play |
| **Thank you.** | Merci. | mehr-see |
| **I'm sorry.** | Désolé. | day-zoh-lay |
| **Excuse me.** | Pardon. | par-dohn |
| **No problem.** | Pas de problème. | pah duh proh-blehm |
| **It's good.** | C'est bon. | say bohn |
| **Goodbye.** | Au revoir. | oh ruh-vwahr |
| **one / two / three** | un / deux / trois | uhn / duh / trwah |
| **four / five / six** | quatre / cinq / six | kah-truh / sank / sees |
| **seven / eight** | sept / huit | seht / weet |
| **nine / ten** | neuf / dix | nuhf / dees |
| **How much is it?** | C'est combien? | say kohn-bee-an |
| **Write it?** | Ecrivez? | ay-kree-vay |
| **Is it free?** | C'est gratuit? | say grah-twee |
| **Included?** | Inclus? | an-klew |
| **Where can I buy / find...?** | Où puis-je acheter / trouver...? | oo pwee-zhuh ah-shuh-tay / troo-vay |
| **I'd like / We'd like...** | Je voudrais / Nous voudrions... | zhuh voo-dray / noo voo-dree-ohn |
| **...a room.** | ...une chambre. | ewn shahn-bruh |
| **...a ticket to ___.** | ...un billet pour ___. | uhn bee-yay poor ___ |
| **Is it possible?** | C'est possible? | say poh-see-bluh |
| **Where is...?** | Où est...? | oo ay |
| **...the train station** | ...la gare | lah gar |
| **...the bus station** | ...la gare routière | lah gar root-yehr |
| **...tourist information** | ...l'office du tourisme | loh-fees dew too-reez-muh |
| **Where are the toilets?** | Où sont les toilettes? | oo sohn lay twah-leht |
| **men / women** | hommes / dames | ohm / dahm |
| **left / right** | à gauche / à droite | ah gohsh / ah drwaht |
| **straight** | tout droit | too drwah |
| **pull / push** | tirez / poussez | tee-ray / poo-say |
| **When does this open / close?** | Ça ouvre / ferme à quelle heure? | sah oo-vruh / fehrm ah kehl ur |
| **At what time?** | À quelle heure? | ah kehl ur |
| **Just a moment.** | Un moment. | uhn moh-mahn |
| **now / soon / later** | maintenant / bientôt / plus tard | man-tuh-nahn / bee-an-toh / plew tar |
| **today / tomorrow** | aujourd'hui / demain | oh-zhoor-dwee / duh-man |

# In a French Restaurant

| | |
|---|---|
| **I'd like / We'd like...** | Je voudrais / Nous voudrions... <br> zhuh voo-dray / noo voo-dree-ohn |
| **...to reserve...** | ...réserver...    ray-zehr-vay |
| **...a table for one / two.** | ...une table pour un / deux. <br> ewn tah-bluh poor uhn / duh |
| **Is this seat free?** | C'est libre?    say lee-bruh |
| **The menu (in English), please.** | La carte (en anglais), s'il vous plaît. <br> lah kart (ahn ahn-glay) see voo play |
| **service (not) included** | service (non) compris <br> sehr-vees (nohn) kohn-pree |
| **to go** | à emporter    ah ahn-por-tay |
| **with / without** | avec / sans    ah-vehk / sahn |
| **and / or** | et / ou    ay / oo |
| **breakfast / lunch / dinner** | petit déjeuner / déjeuner / dîner <br> puh-tee day-zhuh-nay / day-zhuh-nay / dee-nay |
| **special of the day** | plat du jour    plah dew zhoor |
| **specialty of the house** | spécialité de la maison <br> spay-see-ah-lee-tay duh lah may-zohn |
| **appetizers** | hors d'œuvre    or duh-vruh |
| **first course (soup, salad)** | entrée    ahn-tray |
| **main course (meat, fish)** | plat principal    plah pran-see-pahl |
| **bread / cheese** | pain / fromage    pan / froh-mahzh |
| **sandwich / soup** | sandwich / soupe    sahnd-weech / soop |
| **salad** | salade    sah-lahd |
| **meat / chicken** | viande / poulet    vee-ahnd / poo-lay |
| **fish / seafood** | poisson / fruits de mer <br> pwah-sohn / frwee duh mehr |
| **fruit / vegetables** | fruit / légumes    frwee / lay-gewm |
| **dessert** | dessert    day-sehr |
| **mineral water** | eau minérale    oh mee-nay-rahl |
| **tap water** | l'eau du robinet    loh dew roh-bee-nay |
| **(orange) juice** | jus (d'orange)    zhew (doh-rahnzh) |
| **coffee / tea / milk** | café / thé / lait    kah-fay / tay / lay |
| **wine / beer** | vin / bière    van / bee-ehr |
| **red / white** | rouge / blanc    roozh / blahn |
| **glass / bottle** | verre / bouteille    vehr / boo-tay |
| **Cheers!** | Santé!    sahn-tay |
| **More. / Another.** | Plus. / Un autre.    plew / uhn oh-truh |
| **The same.** | La même chose.    lah mehm shohz |
| **The bill, please.** | L'addition, s'il vous plaît. <br> lah-dee-see-ohn see voo play |
| **Do you accept credit cards?** | Vous prenez les cartes?    voo pruh-nay lay kart |
| **tip** | pourboire    poor-bwahr |
| **Delicious!** | Délicieux!    day-lees-yuh |

For more user-friendly French phrases, check out *Rick Steves' French Phrase Book* or *Rick Steves' French, Italian & German Phrase Book*.

# INDEX

INDEX

INDEX

## Explore Europe

At ricksteves.com you can browse through thousands of articles, videos, photos and radio interviews, plus find a wealth of money-saving travel tips for planning your dream trip. And with our mobile-friendly website, you can easily access all this great travel information anywhere you go.

## TV Shows

Preview the places you'll visit by watching entire half-hour episodes of *Rick Steves' Europe* (choose from all 100 shows) on-demand, for free.

# ricksteves.com

*your travel dreams into affordable reality*

## Radio Interviews

Enjoy ready access to Rick's vast library of radio interviews covering travel tips and cultural insights that relate specifically to your Europe travel plans.

## Travel Forums

Learn, ask, share! Our online community of savvy travelers is a great resource for first-time travelers to Europe, as well as seasoned pros.

## Travel News

Subscribe to our free Travel News e-newsletter, and get monthly updates from Rick on what's happening in Europe.

## Classroom Europe®

Check out our free resource for educators with 500 short video clips from the *Rick Steves' Europe* TV show.

Get your FREE **Rick Steves Audio Europe**™ app to enjoy…

- Dozens of self-guided tours of Europe's top museums, sights and historic walks

- Hundreds of tracks filled with cultural insights and sightseeing tips from Rick's radio interviews

- All organized into handy geographic playlists

- For Apple and Android

With Rick whispering in your ear, Europe gets even better.

# Find out more at ricksteves.com

*Gear up for your next adventure at ricksteves.com*

## Light Luggage

Pack light and right with Rick Steves' affordable, custom-designed rolling carry-on bags, backpacks, day packs and shoulder bags.

## Accessories

From packing cubes to moneybelts and beyond, Rick has personally selected the travel goodies that will help your trip go smoother.

## Save time and energy

This guidebook is your independent-travel toolkit. But for all it delivers, it's still up to you to devote the time and energy it takes to manage the preparation and logistics that are essential for a happy trip. If that's a hassle, there's a solution.

## Rick Steves Tours

A Rick Steves tour takes you to Europe's most interesting places with great

guides and small groups. We follow Rick's favorite itineraries, ride in comfy buses, stay in family-run hotels, and bring you intimately close to the Europe you've traveled so far to see. Most importantly, we take away the logistical headaches so you can focus on the fun.

## Join the fun

This year we'll take thousands of free-spirited travelers—nearly half of them repeat customers— along with us on 50 different itineraries, from Athens to Istanbul. Is a Rick Steves tour the right fit for your travel dreams?

Find out at ricksteves.com, where you can also check seat availability and sign up. Europe is best experienced with happy travel partners. We hope you can join us.

**See our itineraries at ricksteves.com**

## BEST OF GUIDES

*Full-color guides in an easy-to-scan format. Focused on top sights and experiences in the most popular European destinations*

Best of England
Best of Europe
Best of France
Best of Germany
Best of Ireland
Best of Italy
Best of Scotland
Best of Spain

## COMPREHENSIVE GUIDES

*City, country, and regional guides printed on Bible-thin paper. Packed with detailed coverage for a multi-week trip exploring iconic sights and venturing off the beaten path*

Amsterdam & the Netherlands
Barcelona
Belgium: Bruges, Brussels,
  Antwerp & Ghent
Berlin
Budapest
Croatia & Slovenia
Eastern Europe
England
Florence & Tuscany
France
Germany
Great Britain
Greece: Athens & the Peloponnese
Iceland
Ireland
Istanbul
Italy
London
Paris
Portugal
Prague & the Czech Republic
Provence & the French Riviera
Rome
Scandinavia
Scotland
Sicily
Spain
Switzerland
Venice
Vienna, Salzburg & Tirol

E BEST OF ROME

Italy's capital, is studded with remnants and floodlit-fountain . From the Vatican to the Colos- ith crazy traffic in between, Rome erful, huge, and exhausting. The he heat, and the weighty history

of the Eternal City where Caesars walked can make tourists wilt. Recharge by tak- ing siestas, gelato breaks, and after-dark walks, strolling from one atmospheric square to another in the refreshing eve- ning air.

*antheon—which dome until the 2,000 years old ver 1,500).*

*thens in the Vat- the humanistic*

*ators fought her, entertaining*

## POCKET GUIDES
*Compact color guides for shorter trips*

Amsterdam
Athens
Barcelona
Florence
Italy's Cinque Terre
London
Munich & Salzburg
Paris
Prague
Rome
Venice
Vienna

## SNAPSHOT GUIDES
*Focused single-destination coverage*

Basque Country: Spain & France
Copenhagen & the Best of Denmark
Dublin
Dubrovnik
Edinburgh
Hill Towns of Central Italy
Krakow, Warsaw & Gdansk
Lisbon
Loire Valley
Madrid & Toledo
Milan & the Italian Lakes District
Naples & the Amalfi Coast
Nice & the French Riviera
Normandy
Northern Ireland
Norway
Reykjavík
Rothenburg & the Rhine
Sevilla, Granada & Southern Spain
St. Petersburg, Helsinki & Tallinn
Stockholm

## CRUISE PORTS GUIDES
*Reference for cruise ports of call*

Mediterranean Cruise Ports
Scandinavian & Northern European
  Cruise Ports

### Complete your library with...

## TRAVEL SKILLS & CULTURE
*Study up on travel skills and gain
insight on history and culture*

Europe 101
Europe Through the Back Door
Europe's Top 100 Masterpieces
European Christmas
European Easter
European Festivals
For the Love of Europe
Italy for Food Lovers
Travel as a Political Act

## PHRASE BOOKS & DICTIONARIES
French
French, Italian & German
German
Italian
Portuguese
Spanish

## PLANNING MAPS
Britain, Ireland & London
Europe
France & Paris
Germany, Austria & Switzerland
Iceland
Ireland
Italy
Scotland
Spain & Portugal

# Photo Credits